Olympia, Tumwater, and Lacey

a pictorial history

by Shanna B. Stevenson

THE DONNING COMPANY PUBLISHERS

Copyright© 1985 Shanna B. Stevenson
Revised edition, 1996.

All rights reserved, including the right to reproduce this work in any form whatsoever without permission in writing from the publisher, except for brief passages in connection with a review. For information write:
    The Donning Company/Publishers
    184 Business Park Drive Suite 106
    Virginia Beach, VA 23462

Beverly Chandler, Project Director
Barbara Bolton, Reprint Project Director

Library of Congress Cataloging-in-Publication Data

Stevenson, Shanna B.
    Lacey, Olympia, and Tumwater
    Bibliography:p.
    Includes index.
    1. Lacey (Wash.)—History—Pictorial Works. 2. Lacey (Wash.)—Description—Views. 3. Olympia (Wash.)—History—Pictorial works. 4. Olympia (Wash.)—Description—Views. 5. Tumwater (Wash.)—History—Pictorial Works. 6. Tumwater (Wash.)—Description—Views.I. Title.
F899.L43S74   1985   979.7'79 86-19813
ISBN 0-89865-497-1

Printed in the United States of America

This beautiful,
illustrated volume has been made possible
thanks to the generous support of

THE
OLYMPIA-TUMWATER
FOUNDATION

MISSION STATEMENT

"To support continuing education of Thurston County
residents and provide and maintain facilities
and lands for public use and enjoyment."

The Olympia-Tumwater Foundation takes great pleasure in making available this updated, limited edition of *Olympia, Tumwater and Lacey: A Pictorial History* authored by noted local historian and writer Shanna B. Stevenson.

By working closely with the author and providing additional historical information gathered from its archives, The Foundation has helped provide an edition that will increase the reader's awareness and insight into the people and their work that shaped our community. It also describes the events that resulted in the formation of The Olympia-Tumwater Foundation.

The Foundation is a private, nonprofit organization that was established in 1950 by descendants of the founder of the Olympia Brewing Company, Leopold T. Schmidt, and other local citizens. The Foundation owns and maintains Tumwater Falls Park and the historic home of Leopold Schmidt, built in 1904, and referred to as "Three Meter." Bordering on the Deschutes River, the Park is a favorite place for scenic walks and picnics and is visited by over 350,000 people annually. "Three Meter," with its spacious grounds that feature the Washington State Centennial Rose Garden, is the site for private parties, as well as business and community functions, and is available for rental.

In addition, through its Memorial Scholarship Program, The Foundation has become the largest endowed source of college scholarships for Thurston County high school students. Since its inception, the program has assisted more than 100 local students by awarding over $200,000 toward their educations. Proceeds from the sale of this book will not only help the Memorial Scholarship Program continue but also will help it to grow.

The Olympia-Tumwater Foundation has been dedicated to serving the community for almost half a century, and by commissioning this publication, the Trustees hope that the historical material it contains will enhance pride in our community's heritage and help foster the desire among future generations to remember our community's past and carry on its history of working for the well-being of its citizens.

Officers and Trustees

Nicholas M. Schmidt*
President

Michael K. Schmidt*
Vice President

Don M. Lee
Vice President/General Manager

James A. Haight*
Treasurer

Stephen J. Bean*
Lynn Brunton*
Jennifer S. Ingham*
James H. Jenner*
Peter G. Schmidt Jr.*
Robert A. Schmidt*
Theodore F. Schmidt*
Susan S. Solie*
Mimi S. Fielding*

*Trustees

Contents

Foreword	9
Preface	11
Acknowledgments	12
Pre-1850 to 1870	15
1870-1890	46
1890-1910	70
Steamboat Travel	106
1910-1930	116
The Capital	142
The Olympia Brewing Company and The Olympia-Tumwater Foundation	156
1930-1950	185
1950-1970	199
1970-1985	217
1985-1995	235
Bibliography	252
Index	253

Foreword

Washington State's capital communities are fortunate to have their collective histories so richly recorded in photographs, manuscripts, family diaries, and other vestiges of our cultural heritage.

Native American cultures, evolving through time, were well adapted to the Southern Puget Sound maritime economy when European explorers recorded their presence and extolled the promises of the land. From these records, pioneers ventured westward and the migration to the Northwest was on. By locating the territorial and state's governmental organization in Olympia, the underlying tone of our community was established for years to come.

The challenges of recording our communities' cultural heritage have been met by Shanna Stevenson, author and historian, in this readable, entertaining, and informative publication.

With *Lacey, Olympia, and Tumwater* at hand we can see the opportunities of the Washington State Centennial in 1989 and the role that Washington State capital communities will play in that celebration of our heritage.

Derek R. Valley
Director
Washington State Capital
Historical Association

Preface

Olympia, the "Pearl of Puget Sound," nestles at the southernmost point of Puget Sound within sight of the magnificent Olympic Mountains, after which it is named, and within the shadow of Mt. Rainier, the most majestic of America's peaks in the lower forty-eight states. Together with its neighbors, Lacey to the northeast and Tumwater to the south, Olympia forms the Capital Community, an area rich in history and heritage. Here on the shores of Puget Sound, settlers formed Washington's first community in Tumwater, established Olympia which has continued to serve as Washington Territorial and State Capital, and settled Lacey where early farmers took advantage of the prairies among the trees to cultivate their crops.

The Capital Community quickly gained prominence as the largest settlement on Puget Sound. It is the first landfall on the Sound from the Cowlitz Trail, over which immigrants traveled from the Columbia River. The tenacity and pioneering spirit of the Simmons-Bush party in Tumwater, the resourcefulness and fortitude of Olympians as they fought to retain the capital, and the daring and innovative spirit of Laceyites as they built a college and racetrack are all reflected in this history.

What comes through is not only the nostalgia of the streetcars on downtown Olympia's brick streets, or the bustle of activity around the falls in Tumwater, or the picturesque train station at Lacey; but also the growth and development of the three communities in the changing fortunes of their history.

Recalling the simpler past of the one-room school, the masted schooner in the harbor, or the steam train to Tenino is certainly a pleasant diversion. However, despite our longing for the days when the "City of Olympia" was flying, the horses were trotting at Woodland, or the streetcars were running out to Tumwater, many of us are still building memories and the later-day photos may jog the memory to "remember when" in the 1980s and 1990s.

Certainly the pride and self-sufficiency of pioneers live on in Tumwater's Historic Park along the falls of the Deschutes and Tumwater Falls Park. Although the advent of the freeway in the 1950s changed the topography of Tumwater, her character lives on in the oasis by the falls.

Out in Lacey, too, the community continues to enlarge and change from the quaint little post office and train station that once were, to the bustling suburban community which ever continues to grow. St. Martin's at 100 is still going strong. A new library, city hall, and office buildings anchor a city center.

Olympia, harkening to its past while creating landmarks for the future, continues to be a vibrant and distinctive Capital City.

Acknowledgments

My thanks to Norman Gallacci who did an excellent job with photographs for the book. My appreciation to Derek Valley of the State Capital Museum, now a branch of the Washington State Historical Society, who shared the copious files of museum photographs with me, and also thanks to the Henderson House Museum staff and the Lacey Museum who opened their collections to me. The late Gordon Newell was kind enough to lend me some of his maritime collection and provided his assistance in solving some historical puzzles.

Mrs. Del Ogden shared her late husband's photographs and Ron Allen copied photographs from his files of longtime Olympia photographer Merle Junk. Gale Johnson, an owner of the Jeffers Studio, provided photos from his "Old Olympia" files. KGY radio, the Port of Olympia, and St. Martin's College all allowed me to copy photographs from their rich store of photographs.

My special appreciation to longtime residents—some of whom are now gone—Catherine Weller, Ruth Drury Beatty, Helen Eskridge Rodman, Ollie Van Slyke, Oakie Armstrong, Carl Reder, Adah Dye, and others who shared memories and photographs with me.

My thanks to The Olympia-Tumwater Foundation for allowing me to use their history-rich archives. Special thanks to Don Lee, P. H. Schmidt, and Peter G. Schmidt Jr. for their assistance. All of the photographs in the chapter on Olympia Brewing Company and The Olympia-Tumwater Foundation are from The Olympia-Tumwater Foundation Collection unless otherwise noted.

My special hope is that the book will give a pleasurable glimpse into the past and provide a guidepost to the future by keeping alive the memory of the heritage of Tumwater, Olympia and Lacey.

lympia, Tumwater, and Lacey

Pre-1850 to 1870

Michael T. Simmons, known as the "Daniel Boone of Washington Territory" for his pioneering efforts, was born in 1814 in Kentucky. Moving westward, he married Elizabeth Kindred in 1836 in Iowa and in 1840 settled in Missouri where he built a grist mill. Joining the westward migration, Simmons was elected Colonel by members of his wagon train in 1844.

He and his family journeyed over the Oregon trail reaching Washougal on the Columbia River in 1845. After reconnoitering the surrounding area, Simmons and a few members of the wagon train ventured northward into what was considered British territory under the direction of the Hudson's Bay Company. Simmons recognized the potential of the power of the falls of the Deschutes and determined to settle nearby, naming the area "New Market."

Simmons was a leader in the effort to create a separate territory from Oregon, served as Indian agent for the Puget Sound Indians, helped organize the first Mason lodge in the state, and was the first postmaster of Nisqually in 1850. Simmons later lived on Big Snookum Bay where he built yet another mill. The beloved pioneer died in 1867 in Lewis County. State Capital Museum photo

The peninsula known as Olympia was "Cheetwoot" to Nisqually Indians at the end of what we now know as Budd Inlet, a favorite shellfish gathering site for many Puget Sound Indians including the Nisqually, Duwamish and Squaxin tribes. "Cheetwoot" meant "bear" in the Nisqually tongue. Evidence exists that the inlet was a meeting place for Indians, and both east and west of the inlet near Olympia were sites of potlatch, the famous Northwest Indian custom in which tribal leaders shared their wealth with neighboring tribal groups.

The falls of the Deschutes River at Tumwater called "Stehtsasamish" by the Nisqually Indians may have been occupied for 500 years or more before the coming of white settlers as a permanent village site for shellfish and salmon harvesting. Spring took the Nisqually to the plains near Lacey called "pollala ilahee" to gather camas (a starchy root vegetable) and other seasonal foodstuffs.

In May 1792 Peter Puget, for whom Puget Sound is named, and a member of the Vancouver party of English explorers visited the site of Olympia but promptly returned to his parent ship, the *Discovery*. The ship's captain, George Vancouver, had also visited the southernmost tip of the sound and realized the fruitlessness of his search for the Northwest Passage.

The British Hudson's Bay Company made a permanent settlement in 1831 at Nisqually north of Olympia. Americans came in July of 1841 when Midshipmen Thomas A. Budd and Henry Eld explored the inlets named for them, as part of the American exploratory expedition. Under the command of Lt. Charles Wilkes, they mapped and named landmarks throughout the Puget Sound region.

In 1845 the area became the northern terminus of the Oregon Trail when Michael T. Simmons and his party defied the Hudson's Bay Company by venturing north of the Columbia River. Simmons called the area that was to become Tumwater, "New Market" which preceded the boundary settlement of 1846 with Great Britain and gave credence to the American claim at the forty-ninth parallel.

Simmons had come from Missouri over the Oregon Trail in 1844 and had first planned to settle in the Rogue River Valley of Oregon. His plan changed because of a ban on black settlers which affected a well-to-do mulatto man, George Bush, a close friend and member of the Simmons party.

While wintering at Washougal near Fort Vancouver, Simmons traveled to the area around the falls of the Deschutes at Tumwater. In late 1845 a party of thirty including the Simmons, Bush, James McAllister, David Kindred, and George Jones families; as well as two single men, Jesse Ferguson and Samuel B. Crockett, set out for the falls, arriving in October. They survived the winter in one cabin eating game and fish and cutting shingles for the Hudson's Bay Company.

Others of the party took claims south of the town site on what was to be known as "Bush Prairie" after George Bush who claimed land there. The farms provided the grain and produce for the mills that eventually sprang up along the falls.

One of the later groups of settlers of 1846, Levi Lathrop Smith, claimed the beaches at Cheetwoot, naming the environs "Smithfield." He and his partner, fellow New Englander Edmund Sylvester, owned jointly the area which is now Olympia. Smith died in 1848 while en route to the Oregon Provisional Legislature.

Under the laws of Oregon Territory, Sylvester inherited the townsite of Olympia. Sylvester, lured to the California gold rush in 1849, returned to Olympia in 1850 and officially platted his new town which he named after the Olympic Mountains, designated by British Capt. John Meares in 1788.

The first industrial development on the sound was at New Market where Simmons built a grist mill to bolt the grain grown on the prairies in 1846-47. The settlement next formed a sawmilling company again using the power of the falls. By 1863 the settlement became known as Tumwater and during the 1860s and 1870s a profusion of small factories sprang up along its banks.

Among the earliest settlers to Olympia were the Catholic missionaries of the Oblates of Mary Immaculate, French clerics who came to the area now known as Priest Point Park to minister to the Indians.

Led by Father Pascal Ricard who established the mission in August 1848, local Indians grew a huge amount of produce and fruit. The priests brought a well-educated influence to the Olympia area until 1860 when they vacated their mission to concentrate on British Columbia ministries.

Olympia prospered despite the Mexican War of 1848 and gold rush in California which drew settlers elsewhere. Named the Port of Entry for Puget Sound in 1851, Olympia was the location of the customs house for the Puget Sound area until 1854. Washington's first newspaper, *The Columbian,* was founded in September 1852 by T. F. McElroy, and agitated for an independent

Elizabeth Kindred Simmons, born in 1820, married Michael Simmons when she was only fifteen years of age. She joined him in the great adventure westward and gave birth to the first white child born on Puget Sound in 1845 after the long journey. Fittingly, he was named Christopher Columbus Simmons.
  After a long and useful life including the rearing of eleven children, Mrs. Simmons died in 1890. State Capital Museum photo

territory north of the Columbia River from Oregon Territory which had been formed in 1848. A new territory was formed in 1853 named "Washington" instead of "Columbia," the name preferred by its settlers.

Isaac Stevens, a West Point graduate and surveyor was sent to the new territory to become its first governor. Arriving in Olympia in November 1853, he named the town provisional capital and set the wheels for government in motion, calling for elections and a territorial legislature for early 1854. That first group set the character of Olympia for the rest of its history—the meeting place of the legislature and the site of government for Washington. They assembled in the largest hall in town which had been built by Edmund Sylvester for Parker-Colter and later known as the Gold Bar Restaurant.

With government launched, Stevens turned to his next obligation as Superintendent of Indian Affairs, which was to extinguish Native American claims to their land so that the way would be open for settlement. Stevens traveled widely throughout Washington in 1854-55 making treaties with Indians. The unsatisfactory outcome of his work coupled with the surge of new settlers brought white-Indian relations to an uprising in 1855-56. Throughout the area blockhouses were built which housed settlers until the uprising was over. Many were located on prairies in Lacey and Olympia. Fortunately bloodshed was at a minimum and although commerce was disrupted by a year spent in blockhouses, the capital community was on its way to growth and prosperity.

Jesse Ferguson was born in Sandusky, Ohio, and, moving successively westward to Illinois and then Missouri, joined the overland pioneer party with Michael T. Simmons.

Ferguson took out a 320-acre donation land claim and later built a blockhouse on his property during the Indian Uprising of 1855-56.

He was a partner in the early mills in Tumwater along the falls of the Deschutes and tried his luck in the California gold rush and the search for the precious metal in the Queen Charlotte Islands.

Ferguson died in 1900. State Capital Museum photo

Pictured are Jesse Ferguson and his daughter on their homestead near Tumwater. Ferguson later donated part of his land for the Union Cemetery where many of Tumwater's earliest pioneers are buried.

Jesse Ferguson married Jane Rutledge in 1850 and together they had five children. Pictured is Sara who was the wife of William Lee. They lived on the original Ferguson claim. Henderson House Museum photo

George Washington Bush came to the Tumwater area in 1845 with the Michael T. Simmons party. Son of a black father and white mother, Bush is known as the most famous of the early black pioneers in the capital area.

Born in Pennsylvania, Bush later moved to the Midwest. He had made a trip to the Pacific Coast on an expedition in 1813-1814 before making the overland journey with the Simmons group.

His presence with Simmons, with whom he was a close friend, helped persuade the party to venture northward to escape the restrictive land laws of Oregon against "men of color" as persons of mixed parentage were known in those days.

Bush had accumulated considerable wealth in Missouri and was well-equipped to start farming on Bush Prairie, as his claim became known. Always willing to share his good fortune with others, Bush was well loved by the early settlers. His farm became a stopping off place between the Cowlitz Landing on the Cowlitz River and the settlements of Olympia and Tumwater. Bush died in 1863 at his home on Bush Prairie. Drawing by Samuel Patrick for the Los Angeles Times; Henderson House Museum photo

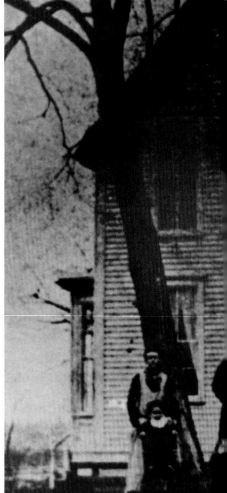

This was one of the early Bush homes on Bush Prairie. George and Isabella James Bush's children were William Owen, Joseph Talbot, Riley Bailey, Henry Sanford, and Jackson January Bush.

The original home had to be torn down in 1970. Henderson House Museum photo.

Another view of the Bush home with members of the Bush family. Henderson House Museum photo

Edmund Sylvester is known as the founder of Olympia. A native of Eastport, Maine, Sylvester came to Oregon in 1843 via the bark Pallas *at the young age of twenty-two. He remained in the Astoria-Portland area for two years but, being a native New Englander, he felt that the salt water climate would restore his ailing health.*

Sylvester took up a claim south of Olympia and his partner, Levi Lathrop Smith, whom he had met in Oregon, settled in what we now know as Olympia. After Smith's death, Sylvester, although owner of the area, did not lay out a town until his return from an ill-fated trip to the California gold fields in 1850.

Sylvester was a far-sighted man visualizing his settlement as a capital and center of timber trade although it did not reach its full potential in his lifetime. State Capital Museum photo

Sylvester erected the showplace of early Olympia along Capitol Way between Seventh and Eighth streets facing the water. The home was the largest in Olympia and Sylvester's strong-minded wife Clara hosted the first meeting of the Woman's Club here in 1883 and housed a number of visiting suffragettes during the fight of Washington women for the right to vote.

The house remained a landmark for many years but was moved in 1961 and later burned. State Capital Museum photo

In 1852 Ira Ward and Smith Hays founded a sawmill on the west side of the upper falls of the Deschutes River in Tumwater using power generated via a flume for two single sash saws. State Capital Museum photo

The Burlingame Mill was located below the lower falls of the Deschutes River as it empties into Puget Sound. The mill utilized the power of the falls to power the boring machinery which made wooden water pipe.

Isaac Burlingame was born in Michigan. He came to Tumwater in 1878, where he worked for the American Pipe Company. He became manager of the company in 1883. In 1885 he organized the Washington Saw and Planing Mill and later moved to Seattle. State Capital Museum photo

The Carter and Biles Tannery was located across the Deschutes River from the Long Bridge, one of the many manufacturers at the mouth of the Deschutes. Tumwater was dubbed the "Lowell of the West," comparing it with the busy manufacturing town of Lowell, Massachusetts.

James and Clark Biles built their homes nearby where the tannery remained until it was purchased for the Olympia Brewery by Leopold Schmidt in 1895. The old brewhouse is still on this site. Henderson House Museum photo

James Biles came to Tumwater in 1853 from a Kentucky plantation. He was among the first immigrants through the Naches Pass.

Biles settled in Tumwater, and like many pioneers served in many civic capacities. State Capital Museum photo

James Biles and a Mr. Lee built the Lee and Biles store on the left of the photo in 1869. The upper floor was used as a dance hall and clubroom. To the right was the Kaifer saloon and home. Next to the Kaifer home was the Wallace Hotel and on the extreme right, the Krantz Hotel, both built during the 1880s. These all overlooked the falls along the Deschutes River in Tumwater.

On June 19, 1886, James Biles was named Postmaster of Tumwater and at that time the post office was installed at the general merchandise store of Lee & Biles. State Capital Museum photo

George Gelbach came from Pennsylvania to Washington Territory in 1870. He established a flouring mill along the falls of the Deschutes River.

He and his wife are pictured here in a formal portrait. State Capital Museum photo

Gelbach's Washington Flour Mills occupied a prominent place along the middle falls of the Deschutes until 1890 when the location was sold to the Olympia Electric Light and Power Company. State Capital Museum photo

The Crosby Flouring Mill, also known as the Lincoln Flouring Mill, is shown here looking north from Tumwater across the Long Bridge to Olympia.

Built in 1861 by Clanrick Crosby, the five-story mill was powered by the falls of the Deschutes River which operated a four-stone grist mill which had a fifty-bushel per day capacity.

The landmark burned in 1904. State Capital Museum photo

Nathaniel Crosby III was born in 1836, one of a family of sea captains from Massachusetts. His father, Nathaniel II, had come to the northwest after being sent on the O.C. Raymond with supplies for northwest settlers.

The entire family came on the brig Grecian to Puget Sound in 1849 to settle. Nathaniel III's uncle Clanrick bought Michael T. Simmons' claim and built a number of businesses in Tumwater including the flouring mill and store. Nathaniel III remained in Tumwater but his father journeyed to China where he later died. Nathaniel III was the grandfather of entertainer Bing Crosby. State Capital Museum photo

The Crosby House was built in 1858 by Nathaniel Crosby III for his bride Cordelia Jane Smith. The house has been continuously occupied since it was built and still has many original furnishings and a unique hand-hewn handrail leading upstairs. Members of the Schmidt family and descendants of the Crosby family purchased the house in 1941 in the name of the Daughters of the Pioneers of Washington, Chapter 4. The house is now owned by the City of Tumwater and is operated by the Daughters of the Pioneers of Washington, Chapter 4, who continue to own the contents of the house and retain a life estate in the property. The house was placed on the National Register of Historic Places in 1978 as part of the Tumwater Historic District. State Capital Museum photo

The Crosby Store was built in 1852 by Clanric Crosby at the north end of Deschutes Way near the Nathaniel Crosby House. Pictured here are Tumwater residents clustered around proprietor Nathaniel who is without a hat. State Capital Museum photo

Shown is a view of the Long Bridge, open, looking toward Tumwater. A road to Olympia from Tumwater was opened in 1853 and in 1850 this wagon bridge connecting Olympia and Tumwater was built.

The bridge measured 1150 feet long, fifteen feet wide and was six to ten-feet above mean tide level. A forty-foot long bridge section over the Deschutes River channel rotated to allow ship traffic through the twenty-foot wide channel passage. State Capital Museum photo.

Louis Bettman came to Olympia in 1853 from Bavaria, Germany. He opened with his brothers Mose and Sig Bettman a general merchandise store. Located at Second and Main streets, the store offered a wide variety of items and even traded for vouchers from the early Tumwater mills before money was in common supply.

Bettman later located his store at 410 Main Street now known as Capitol Way. State Capital Museum photo

The Bettman's first store at Second and Main with its varied merchandise is pictured here with the Bettman brothers, proprietors. State Capital Museum photo

Pacific House, shown here in its declining years, was built in 1855 and operated in early years by William Cock. Located at Main and Third streets, the hostelry was a favorite gathering place for Olympians and visiting legislators alike. Its popularity increased when it was taken over by Rebecca Howard in 1860. "Aunt Becky," as she was known, was a black woman who was an excellent cook and hostess. Her death in 1881 was widely mourned. State Capital Museum photo

The drawbridge to the west side of Olympia was first built in 1869. West Olympia was known originally as "Marshville," after Edmund Marsh, whose land claim encompassed much of the land across Budd Inlet from downtown Olympia.
   The bridge was built on pilings and subject to wood-destroying elements. The drawbridge did not work well from the time it was built.
   The steep Harrison hill was re-graded in 1880 and a new bridge erected in 1890 which also proved unsatisfactory. The present bridge was built in 1921. State Capital Museum photo

Like most pioneer communities Olympia was anxious to organize its own school. School first opened in November 1852, and was taught by A. W. Moore. The district began as a part of Lewis County prior to the origin of Thurston County. A tax was levied in Olympia in 1852-1853 and enough money was raised to build the cabin and leave $400 for school expenses. Twenty-one children were of school age and half of them attended. Unfortunately, heavy snows collapsed the roof of the building the first winter and school met elsewhere. The building was also the first meeting site of the Methodist Church in Olympia. Other early schools were at Nisqually, Ruddell, and Bush Prairie.

This new frame schoolhouse was built in August 1855 on the site of the collapsed building, the southeast corner of Sixth and Franklin. It was later used as a courthouse and here as the Olympian office. State Capital Museum photo

This was the first Bush Prairie school, organized in 1852 on the David Kindred claim. Henderson House Museum photo

Here is the second Bush Prairie school, built about 1910 and shown shortly after completion. Photo courtesy of Mrs. Ruth Beatty

The Congregationalist Church was dedicated in 1874. Services were held in the Masonic Hall until the building was completed. Early ministers were the Rev. C. A. Hunting, G. W. Skinner, and D. Thomas. State Capital Museum photo

The first Presbyterian Church to be organized in Washington Territory convened November 12, 1854 in the cooperage shop of Wood's Brewery at Fifth Avenue on Columbia in Olympia. The Rev. George Whitworth conducted services until 1860 when the Rev. R. J. Evans took over the pastorage.

Dedicated in 1860, the church was located at the corner of Legion and Franklin and seated 350 people. Other early ministers were the Rev. J. R. Thompson, the Rev. W. B. See, and the Rev. T. J. Lamont.

The congregation was federated with the First Congregationalist Church to form the United Churches in 1916. State Capital Museum photo

This Methodist church was built in 1856 by Rev. John DeVore at the southeast corner of Fourth and Adams.

The Methodists were an active group in early Olympia. Rev. DeVore sought funds from local businessmen and when he approached Captain Clanrick Crosby, the wily businessman told DeVore he could have all the lumber he could carry and raft in one day for free to build his church. Crosby did not suspect the strength and tenacity of the young minister who old settlers say carried out 30,000 feet of lumber that day—enough to build his church.

The Methodists exchanged their original lot in 1890 for lots on Fifth and Adams and moved to the southwest corner of that intersection in 1894. State Capital Museum photo

Rev. John F. DeVore came to the Northwest in 1853. In his thirty-five years with the Puget Sound District, he pioneered churches in Steilacoom, Tumwater, Seattle and Tacoma and was an elder of the district. He died in 1889. State Capital Museum photo

Samuel Percival, a native of Massachusetts, served in many sea-going capacities before settling in San Francisco in 1851 where he operated a store. He and his wife Lurana Ware Percival came to Olympia January 1, 1853 aboard the bark Sarah Warren with Capt. A. B. Gove and operated a store for the Kendall Company. He later operated his own business at Main and Second streets in Olympia where he stayed in business until 1876. T. N. Ford was his partner.

He also built and operated a sawmill on Percival Creek. Percival Landing in Olympia is also named for the Percival family, long-time steamboat ticketing agents. State Capital Museum photo

This photo from the 1870s shows the Percival Home, the showplace of the west side of Olympia. The house was built in 1874 by contractor Benjamin Harned.

The house boasted a small coal grate in each room and many old-timers remember gala dances on the third floor of the house. After Samuel Percival died in the early 1890s, the house was occupied by Governor Mead and during World War I it was a maternity home under the direction of a stern Miss Maxwell. State Capital Museum photo

This is a view of the Percival Home looking eastward across Deschutes Waterway to downtown Olympia. State Capital Museum photo

Daniel Richardson Bigelow was one of Olympia and Thurston County's most outstanding residents.

He was born in Belleville, New York, in 1824 and graduated from Harvard Law School in 1849.

Fearing the loss of his eyesight, he journeyed westward in 1849 settling for a short while at Portland in 1850 and sailing to Olympia in 1851.

He built a law office in the same month as his arrival and took out a 350-acre donation land claim on the east side of Olympia.

Because of his legal expertise, he was invaluable in assisting the neophyte governments of the area. In 1852 he helped establish the boundaries of the newly formed Thurston County and later served as treasurer, justice of the peace, auditor, and prosecuting attorney. He also helped establish Olympia as the county seat. In 1853 he helped rewrite the laws of Oregon Territory of which Olympia was then a part.

He was a defender of human rights including being the leader in granting George Bush property rights in the Washington Legislature. He was an advocate of temperance, suffrage, and education, serving a number of terms as superintendent of schools and heading the effort to locate a Methodist college in Olympia.

He was a member of the first legislature for Washington Territory in 1854 and outlived all other members of that legislature when he died in 1905. State Capital Museum photo

Isaac Ingalls Stevens, first Washington territorial governor, was a dynamic and controversial figure in early Olympia and Washington history.

Born in 1818 in Marble Ridge, Massachusetts, he attended the prestigious Phillips Academy and went on to graduate at the head of all of his classes at West Point and first in his graduating class.

He served in the Mexican War and in the spring of 1853 was named governor of Washington Territory by President Franklin Pierce. A dynamo of ambition, Stevens was named superintendent of Indian affairs, to negotiate treaties to obtain land rights to all of Washington Territory; and head of the railroad survey for the northern transcontinental route of the railroad.

Stevens fulfilled all of these jobs, although his treaties with the Indians, done in a whirlwind fashion, helped precipitate the Indian Uprising of 1855-56 when his declaration of martial law in Olympia and Fort Steilacoom helped to further alienate him from some factions.

He served two terms in Congress starting in 1857 as a delegate from Washington Territory and the state and territory owes him a debt as its principal advocate and organizer during that period.

Stevens died a hero's death at Chantilly in 1862. State Capital Museum photo

Margaret Lyman Hazard Stevens came from a prominent New England family and arrived in Olympia in 1854 with her four children to be at her husband's side. She had married Isaac Stevens in 1841. Mrs. Stevens was a gracious hostess and brought an air of civility to the frontier town. After her husband's death, she stayed in Olympia for a time, later moving back to the East Coast where she died in 1914. State Capital Museum photo

Fort Eaton was one of the many blockhouses built in the area during the Indian Uprising of 1855-56. The Uprising generated by eastern Washington tribes erupted on the west side of the mountains with a flurry when two men were killed near Puyallup, in October 1855. Business, farming, and immigration stopped as all available men were recruited to build protective blockhouses and as they joined the volunteers. Twelve blockhouses were built in the Olympia environs.

Fort Eaton, built by the Freedom Community, was one of the outlying fortifications. Joseph Conner, William White, Alijah O'Neil, A. W. Stewart, and Marcus McMillan built the fort in December 1855 near where Mullan Road intersects with the Yelm Highway east of Olympia.

The sixteen log buildings were connected by a high stockade in a square configuration. This was called a Kentucky type station, perhaps inspired by the Chambers family who had lived in the area, one-time Kentucky residents. Eight families lived in the fortification during the fighting which lasted through 1856.

The blockhouse was a play area for children until its removal in 1882. The site of the blockhouse was marked by the Freedom Community in 1939 and the marker was recently restored. State Capital Museum photo

Lacey also had a number of early schools created because of America's drive toward educating her children. One of the earliest was the Ruddell school, an eighteen foot by twenty-four foot structure, near what is now the Pioneer Cemetery. The Freedom Community founded a school in 1854 on the Marcus McMillan Farm in the area now known as Kagy Road. Another school was built on Wood's Prairie on the Isaac Wood claim in 1856 and a frame school built there in 1858.

Pictured here is an early four-room structure erected on land donated from their farm by the Fleetwood family near the present Lacey School District Headquarters, circa 1880. Lacey Historical Museum photo

Chambers Farmhouse, pictured here, was part of the David Chambers farm, later a golf course and also the site of Panorama City.

The Thomas Chambers family came to Washington Territory in 1848. They were natives of Belfast, Ireland and had resided in a number of states before coming to Washington. Letitia Chambers was a cousin of Andrew Jackson for whom the family had worked. Thomas and Letitia's children, Thomas, James, A. H., Mary, George, David, and Walter, all settled in the area and many places carry their name including Chambers Lake and Chambers Prairie. Photograph of a painting by Edward Lange in the State Capital Museum Collection

John Miller Murphy and his paper, the Washington Standard, *were fixtures in Olympia for over a half century.*

Murphy crossed the plains from Indiana in 1850 with his sister, Mrs. George Barnes, first settling in Portland, Oregon. An orphan, Murphy learned the printing trade there. Barnes and Miller moved to Olympia in 1851.

In 1860, Murphy began his Washington Standard, *a Republican voice in the capital which continued over fifty years. Murphy also served in many capacities in the community including being the first territorial auditor and a city councilman.*

The Standard *continued publication until 1913. Murphy died in 1915. State Capital Museum photo*

The Washington Standard *office, shown circa 1885, was located at the corner of Washington and Second streets. State Capital Museum photo*

The Washington Standard *interior is pictured circa 1900. Notice the wooden type fonts and pot-bellied stove. Murphy trained his daughters in the printing trade, being a believer in suffrage and rights for women. State Capital Museum photo*

John Melvin Hawk for whom Hawk's Prairie is named was in reality the fourth resident of the prairies. Native Americans passed over the prairie on their annual camas digging expeditions in the spring.

Early white settlers to the area were the Tyrell and Baker families. Hawk crossed the plains in 1852 first settling in the Portland, Oregon area. He later settled in the area known now as Hawk's Prairie on a claim adjacent to the Himes family, also early pioneers. Photo courtesy of Mrs. H. A. Hawk

Mary Olney Brown came west with her husband Benjamin Brown in 1846. They operated an orchard and later moved to Olympia where Brown and a neighbor, John French, built the long wharf on the west side where timber spars were loaded.

Mrs. Brown not only gave birth to eleven children but was a writer and poetess as well as being a respected nurse in the community.

She also raised her voice in the cause of women's suffrage before the Washington Territorial Legislature as early as 1866 and continued to work toward that goal in ensuing years. State Capital Museum photo

Old Betsy was a member of the Nisqually Tribe, the indigenous peoples to the bays and inlets around Olympia. She was a common sight before the turn of the century as she dug and delivered clams and oysters to housewives in Olympia. She lived on the shore below the present capitol and lived to be over 100 years of age. State Capital Museum photo

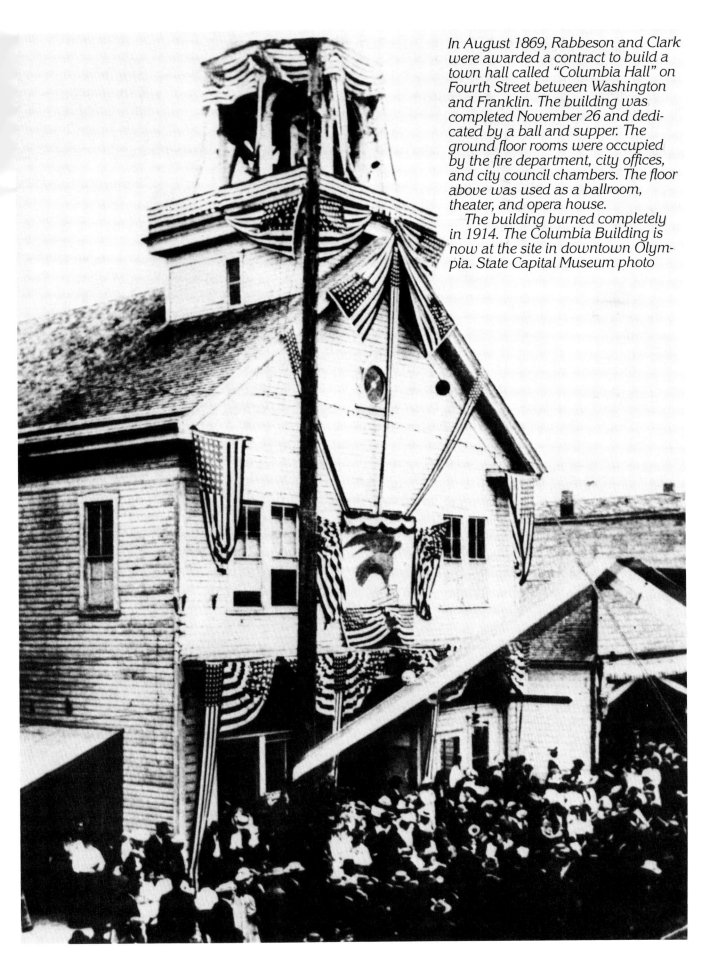

In August 1869, Rabbeson and Clark were awarded a contract to build a town hall called "Columbia Hall" on Fourth Street between Washington and Franklin. The building was completed November 26 and dedicated by a ball and supper. The ground floor rooms were occupied by the fire department, city offices, and city council chambers. The floor above was used as a ballroom, theater, and opera house.

The building burned completely in 1914. The Columbia Building is now at the site in downtown Olympia. State Capital Museum photo

The Capitol was arrayed in bunting and evergreens for Statehood Day, November 18, 1889. Elisha Ferry was inaugurated as the first governor of Washington State. "Old Olympia" photo from the Jeffers Studio Collection

1870-1890

The decade of the 1870s was the "Era of the Railroad" for the capital area. The title of terminus for the Northern Pacific Railroad was a coveted one among communities up and down Puget Sound. It was even more important for Olympia whose civic prominence rested on its ability to keep the capital and continue its importance as a trade center.

With characteristic boosterism Olympians formed the Olympia Branch Railroad Company and proceeded to purchase a large tract of land southeast of town in what is now the Watershed Park area. This 240 acres was donated to the Northern Pacific to lure it to Olympia. Indeed Olympians received written confirmation that Olympia was to be the terminus in 1871. The railroad was no less important to Tumwater which had become known as the "Lowell of the Pacific" comparing it to Lowell, Massachusetts, because of its wide range of small manufacturers which clustered around the water power of the Deschutes Falls. A railroad would enlarge the range of their exports of prunes, wood, furniture, leather goods, and flour.

The hopes of Olympians and Tumwaterites alike were dashed by the announcement in 1873 that the Northern Pacific had bypassed Olympia in favor of what was then but a small village—Tacoma—as its terminus.

Undaunted, Olympians decided to gather in their town square to build their own railroad to Tenino, fifteen miles distant and the closest connection with the main line of the Northern Pacific. Thursday of each week was set aside as railroad day and the first turnout yielded over 300 men, and seventy-five women came to provide nourishment for the hungry workers. Bonds were sold for various associations of railroad promoters and by 1878 the narrow gauge line was complete.

A gala celebration topped by free excursions to Tenino was the order of opening day in August. Rates were twelve and a half cents from Olympia to Tumwater and a dollar to Tenino. The line terminated after crossing the tide flats at the end of the Fourth Street bridge at Marshville, as the west side of Olympia was once called.

The decade of the 1880s was marked with civic improvements and prosperity, capped with the proclamation of statehood in 1889.

Although the railroad was a problem for Olympia and Tumwater, Woodland, as Lacey was known in early years, fared better. With the completion of the main line

Although Olympia was by-passed by the Northern Pacific in 1873 and built their own branch line to Tenino, track finally arrived outside the city limits in 1890 and trains began running in 1891. State Capitol Museum photo

through the area, the Wood family donated land for a station and the area officially became known as "Woodland" as the name on the station proudly proclaimed.

Education became a primary concern in the area when the Union Academy opened in 1879, followed by the Sisters of Charity Providence Academy located at Ninth and Columbia downtown. That same order built the first St. Peter's Hospital on land donated by the city at the corner of Eleventh and Columbia in 1887.

With the completion of many schools and churches, traditionally the realm of females, the pioneer women turned their sights to other matters. Organized in 1871, the Olympia Woman Suffrage Association, headed by the dynamic Mrs. A. H. H. Stuart, led the way to gaining the right to vote for women in Washington in 1883 and kept it in force until 1887.

The 1880s were also the era of extensive civic improvements: the installation of a city water system in Olympia and a new bridge to Tumwater.

Although rail service had extended through Olympia to Tumwater and Lacey, waterborne traffic continued to be the best means of transportation up and down the sound.

The City of Olympia attempted to remedy the problem of mudflats in the Olympia harbor at low tides. A dredge from Oregon, the *Umatilla*, was hired but failed to accomplish any significant deepening of the harbor and cost the city $800. Again the long wharf to deep water appeared to be the answer and in 1885 a wharf 4,798 feet long was built on 927 piles extending from the foot of Main (now Capitol Way) out to deep water to handle steamer traffic.

The stimulus of forthcoming statehood and favorable economic conditions brought a flurry of building to Olympia with the Woodruff Block and Chambers Block in 1887, and the Odd Fellows Hall in 1889.

The bill admitting Washington as a state was signed in by President Fillmore and the constitutional convention was set for July 4 in Olympia. The citizens of Olympia in enterprising style raised $2500 for an addition to the old wooden capitol (built in 1855) to house the convention.

Perhaps readying itself for another difficult fight to keep the capital, Olympia instituted a wide range of improvements. The Olympia and Tumwater Railway began to run its carriages to Tumwater, along Fourth

Building the railroad bed for a logging road on the Port Townsend and Southern Railroad is featured here.

The Port Townsend and Southern purchased the trackage that Olympians had built from Olympia to Tenino and sought to build a railroad to Port Townsend along the water adjacent to Hood Canal. That plan never materialized although some new track was built, about 1890. Photo from the Joseph M. Bailey Collection, Washington State Library

and on the east side. Sunset Telephone-Telegraph Company was chartered. Below ground the Olympia Water Company was laying mains and installing hydrants, while above Western Union Telegraph was erecting poles and wires for an incandescent system of electric lighting which brought a true metropolitan character to the city.

The crowning event of the decade and perhaps the early history of the capital community was the declaration and celebration of statehood in November 1889. Officially declared on November 11, the formal celebration took place on November 18, 1889. Welcomed with cannonades on the 11th, statehood was commemorated with a huge parade on the 18th which included dignitaries, bands, carriages and pioneers. The old wooden capitol was aglow in bunting and was witness to an outpouring of patriotism under the direction of newly named state governor Elisha P. Ferry. He reviewed the militia from the new and ornate Woodruff Building, attended a reception at the Columbia Hall and danced at the first inaugural ball held at the equally elegant Odd Fellow Hall.

Washington was now a state and Olympia was its crowning glory!

This was the Olympia Cornet Band in 1872 at a German Picnic at the fairground. Pictured are Pete Ouelette—snare drum; Nat Crosby—bass drum; Charlie Morre—trombone; Theodore Brown—tenor; Ole Simenson—baritone; Charlie White—tuba; Back row: E. B. Osborn—cornet; Eltney Van Epps—cornet; Cooper—alto; Havier Hosneder and wife from the East Side Brewery; Back of steps: Herman Hadlen and wife, beer hall owners; Mrs. Hagemyer with big white apron.

The band was organized in 1857 with ten brass instruments ordered from San Francisco, and a teacher was hired from Portland to instruct the group. State Capital Museum photo

Governor Elisha Ferry and his military staff are shown in the early 1870s.

Ferry was a native of Michigan who was admitted to practice law there. He went on to become mayor of Waukegan, Illinois and Illinois State Bank commissioner. In 1869 he was appointed surveyor general for Washington Territory by President Grant who also named him territorial governor in 1872 and reappointed him to that post in 1876. He practiced law for a time in Seattle and was elected state governor in 1889. After serving in that capacity until 1893, Ferry died in 1895. State Capital Museum photo

Dr. Nathaniel Ostrander is pictured with one of his many descendants.

Dr. Ostrander crossed the plains with his family in 1852 and settled in Cowlitz County. In 1872 he moved to Tumwater and opened an office by a drugstore. He was a prominent physician in Olympia and Tumwater. The first probate judge of Cowlitz County and a state legislator, he was also a member of the Monticello Convention of 1853, which helped agitate for the creation of Washington Territory.

Nathaniel Ostrander was married to Eliza Jane Yantis and together they had ten girls and one son. Mrs. Ostrander died in 1899, Dr. Ostrander in 1902. State Capital Museum photo

Dr. and Mrs. Ostrander built this home in 1887. Ostrander sub-platted the block bounded by Franklin, Adams, Eighth, and Ninth streets in Olympia and built homes for his large family all around that block. The new Olympia Timberland Library now occupies that area. State Capital Museum photo

Captain Woodbury Doane was a native of Maine who joined the California gold rush in 1849 and later made his way to Olympia and Puget Sound as mate on the steamer Eliza Anderson.

Captain Doane made the tiny Olympia Oyster famous and his oyster pan roast was the toast of early Olympia. In fact, the Olympia oyster was dubbed a "succulent lobbyist for retaining the capital in Olympia" because of its persuasive power on the palate of legislators.

In fact, during the votes on the location of the capital, Olympia residents traveled statewide hosting oyster dinners and touting the merits of Olympia as the capital city.

The dapper Mr. Doane died in 1903. State Capital Museum photo

Doane's Oyster House was located between Main (Capitol Way) and Washington on Fifth Street.

Doane's Pan Roast Recipe was "Wash oysters well, put in pan and let come to a simmer, then add a good chunk of butter, then three or four tablespoonsful of catsup and a little pepper but no salt. Toasted bread."

The restaurant was a mecca for legislators and townspeople often serving over sixty gallons of oysters daily. State Capital Museum photo

The area west of Main Street in south Olympia in 1878 is shown. State Capital Museum photo

The Nathan Eaton family hosted a picnic for neighbors in 1871.
Nathan Eaton came in 1853 to the Yelm prairie. His property was the site of Fort Eaton blockhouse during the Indian Uprising of 1855-56.
Nathan Eaton established the first sawmill away from Puget Sound, building a millchase on Eaton Creek to power a sash saw. He was a photographer who built a daguerrotype studio in 1862. He also introduced the first mowing machine into the district. Eaton married Lestina Himes of the pioneer Lacey family in 1872. He sold his property in 1882 and died a year later in Yelm. State Capital Museum photo

William O. Bush, son of pioneer George Bush organized an exhibit for the Centennial Exhibition in Philadelphia in 1876 of the products of his prairie farm. The presentation served to acquaint sightseers with the qualities of Washington State. Bush received a gold medal for the exhibit and took the production to other fairs in Chicago, Buffalo, and St. Louis advertising the farming prospects of Thurston County.

The display featured a wide array of agricultural products including thirty-one varieties of wheat, oats, barley, flax, hemp, buckwheat, corn, potatoes, tobacco, vegetables, and fruit, all grown on Bush Prairie. State Capital Museum photo

Students of the Olympia Central School gathered for a photograph in 1882.

The building at Union and Washington was occupied until 1861 by the Puget Sound Wesleyan Institute organized in 1858. The Olympia Union Academy succeeded the institution in the same building. After the Methodists left the structure, it was used as a ladies academy, then purchased by Thurston County and used as a courthouse until 1870. The Central School was located in the structure with additions from 1875 to 1894. State Capital Museum photo

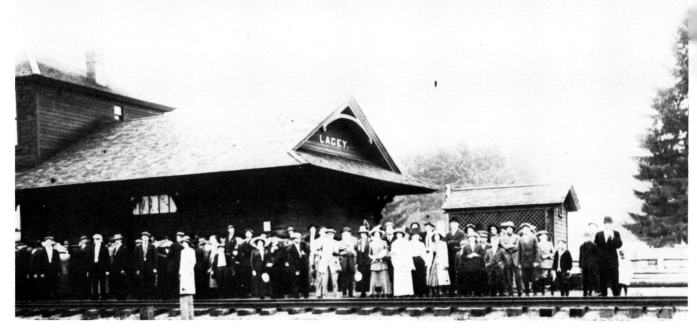

Lacey residents are shown at the railroad station which stood at the present site of Lacey Plywood. State Capital Museum photo

Sisters of Charity built a hospital on land given by Edmund Sylvester and were open for business in 1887. The hospital provided welcome care not only for local residents but was especially important for the victims of catastrophic accidents in surrounding logging camps and mills. Additions were made in 1910, 1913, and 1917.

The building was torn down to accommodate expansion on the Capitol Campus in the 1920s and the hospital was moved to the west side of Olympia. The building stood at the site of the totem pole on the present grounds. State Capital Museum photo

The Providence Academy established by the Sisters of Charity of Providence was built in 1882 at Ninth and Columbia in Olympia. The school was requested by Fr. Hylebos of Tacoma and began as the St. Amable Academy in 1881 in temporary quarters. The boarding and day school was built by Mother Joseph of Providence and became St. Michael's School in April 1926. State Capital Museum photo

59

Members of the Eastman family were photographed in front of their Tumwater home in 1889. Charles Eastman came to Tumwater in 1864 from New Hampshire. He was a blacksmith and served as a postmaster. Henderson House Museum photo

The Burntrager Grocery in Tumwater is shown here in 1882. Henderson House Museum photo

The Toklas & Kaufman store was built in 1883 by Charles Williams as the Olympic Block. It was a City of Paris store for a number of years. They also had stores in Aberdeen and Seattle.

The store was later purchased by George Mottman who started as a clerk for Toklas and Kaufman. Mottman added a third floor in 1910, and Mottman's remained in business until 1967.

The most famous landmark in Olympia mercantile history, the store was recently placed on the National Register of Historic Places. State Capital Museum photo

The Columbia Building was located at the northeast corner of Fourth and Columbia shown here in 1886. Mrs. Mary Munn ran the hotel. She was the mother of Emma Hunter, Ida Curtin, Celia Littlejohn, Charles Besse, Maggie Moyer, Burt Besse, and May Tunin. She was born in 1837 and died in 1922. She also ran the Tilley House at the northwest corner of Fifth and Washington and the Carlton House at Third and Columbia, other prominent hostelries in Olympia. State Capital Museum photo

This drawing of early Olympia shows two of its earliest mercantiles.

Gustave Rosenthal came in 1863 to Olympia and set up his store just north of Fourth and Main. He stocked dry goods, clothing, hardware, crockery, glassware, and farm implements.

He was active in developing the Natches Pass road to Olympia, setting up coal mining, and promoting the lumber trade with San Francisco. In addition, he was an enthusiastic supporter of the railroad and the export of oysters. State Capital Museum photo

Pamela Case Hale was named superintendent of schools in 1882. She was a founder of the State Teachers Association and a founding member of the Women's Club. Her husband Calvin H. Hale was a prominent Olympia legislator and superintendent of Indian affairs. State Capital Museum photo

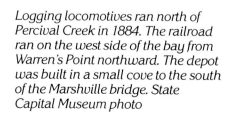

Logging locomotives ran north of Percival Creek in 1884. The railroad ran on the west side of the bay from Warren's Point northward. The depot was built in a small cove to the south of the Marshville bridge. State Capital Museum photo

The county land office was located at Main (Capitol Way) and Eighth in 1884. The Federal Building is now at that location. The Wells Fargo Office is to the left of the Land Office. Chester Manville stands before his law office and leaning against the window is A. J. Munson, proprietor of a variety store. State Capital Museum photo

In 1885, the members of the Uniform Rank of the Knights of Pythias at Olympia were: Back row—John Hawk, Clayton Aldred, Milo Root, Frank Snyder, E. O. Free, Bert Wright. Front row—Gus Harris; Prof. W. H. Roberts; Governor Semple; H. Cusack; and Sam McClelland, fire chief.

The fraternal order of the Knights of Pythias began in Olympia in 1884 and met in the Odd Fellows Hall. In 1893 they had their own hall in the Stuart Building at Main and Sixth (now the old Miller store) and later moved to the Odd Fellows Hall. State Capital Museum photo

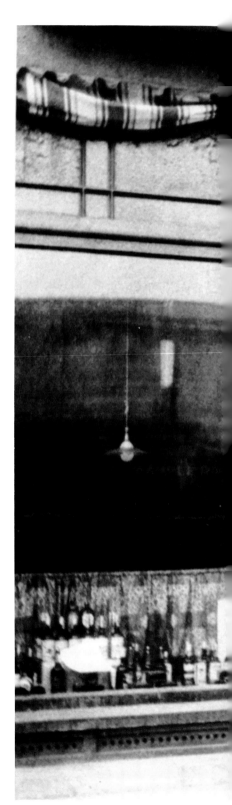

Sam Woodruff was born in China in 1858 and later returned to Olympia where he was a printer and bookseller. In 1889 he also developed the Woodruff Addition on the west side of Olympia, after he purchased the Marsh donation claim. Woodruff Park on the West Side is named for him. Sam Woodruff also developed the town of Gate. *State Capital Museum photo*

The Woodruff Building, also known as the Labor Temple, is located on the west side of Capitol Way between Fourth and State. Built as a two-story structure in 1887 by Sam Woodruff, it housed some of Olympia's early businesses. Van Epps Music was located here and Michael O'Conner had a stationery store with a post office in the rear of the store. Many fraternal and patriotic organizations used this hall as a meeting place and many speakers addressed groups from the balcony. Governor Ferry reviewed militia from there on November 18, 1889 and President Harrison spoke from the second floor on a visit to Olympia. *State Capital Museum photo*

The Odd Fellows Halls was built in 1888 at the corner of Fifth and Main. Dr. Ostrander is at the corner in this photograph. The building burned in 1936.

The first Washington Territorial Odd Fellows Lodge was organized in 1855 in Olympia as Lodge No. 1. The lodge was disbanded during the early 1860s and later reorganized in 1867. The lodge purchased land for a cemetery in 1869 east of Tumwater where many pioneers are buried.

The Odd Fellows are now located on West Fourth in the Barnes Building. State Capital Museum photo

Participants in an operetta in June 1888 were Anne Lansdale, Filoy Frost, Addie Burntrager, Edith Burntrager, Lizzie Burntrager, Mrs. Sam Percival, Louise Ayer, Rena Cavanaugh, and Solie Hartsuck. State Capital Museum photo

Citizens of Olympia and Washington celebrate statehood.

"At 10:30 Grand Marshal Van Epps and aides began forming the procession. It was headed by Mayor Gowey and city officials and followed by the Governor and ex-Governor and the incoming State and retiring Territorial officers in carriages. Then came the First Regiment band, the Pioneers of Washington, the Seattle drum corps, Companies B, C, D and E and three troops of cavalry of the Washington National Guards, the Knights of Pythias, the Tacoma band, the Mason Rifles, Gross Bros.' employees with badges and citizens in carriages, on horses and afoot.... The Capitol building had been beautifully decorated for the occasion. Flags, bunting and evergreens covered the whole portico, and the stage erected in front. Above all appeared a streamer bearing the words, 'Isaac I. Stevens, first in the hearts of the people of Washington Territory, Elisha P. Ferry, first in the hearts of the people of the State of Washington.' In front of the speaker's stand was another legend which was Greek to all but the old settlers. It ran: 'Chinook quanisum ancotty, alti che chaco alki,' which by liberal translation may be rendered 'Living hitherto in the past, we now begin to live in the future.' At the rear of the speaker's stand was a table on which stood a stuffed gray eagle, and a pretty bouquet... as the hour hand approached twelve the Tacoma band ... struck up 'America', that grand old anthem which always sends such a thrill through the hearts of all true Americans." Washington Standard, November 20, 1889. Schmidt House Photo Collection

The Capitol City Band posed on the main steps of the Olympia Hotel. The band was organized in December 1890. State Capital Museum photo

1890-1910

The decade of the 1890s started off in regal style in Olympia with the opening of the new Olympia Hotel. The multi-storied, towered structure had grand verandas overlooking the water. The hotel was part of the continuing effort of Olympians to keep legislators content in comfortable lodgings. Unfortunately, the grand structure burned in 1904.

At long last the railroads were coming to town as the Union Pacific and Northern Pacific both finalized plans to provide service to Olympia. The Northern Pacific required construction of a tunnel under Seventh Street and the first train from the Northern Pacific came through the tunnel in 1891.

The Olympia Light & Power Company built a generator at the middle falls of the Deschutes in Tumwater in 1890, while the Olympia, Tumwater & Brighton Park Motor Railway had street cars running on its four-mile track out to Tumwater to the Hazard Stevens Elk Farm at the falls. The generating facility was in use until 1954.

A building boom accompanied the good times in the early years of the new decade. Olympia residents voted bonds for three new schools—Lincoln and Washington in 1891, followed in 1893 by Garfield.

Plans for a grand new courthouse were under way in 1891 when the county commissioned architect Willis Ritchie to design a new courthouse opposite the town square. His building executed in Chuckanut sandstone was a fitting one for the state capital.

The 1890s were a period of growth and development and in 1891 the name of Woodland was officially changed to Lacey. By that year Woodland had its own post office but difficulties arose because a town on the Columbia River had the same name. An Olympia attorney and land developer, O. C. de Lacey, took the initiative and petitioned post office authorities to rename the Woodland Post Office as the Lacey Post Office. Papers were drawn up in a lawyerly fashion and in June 1891 the name was officially changed. The name of the railroad station was changed later in the decade. Unfortunately, little is known about de Lacey after he left his name on the area.

Major occupations of early Lacey were agricultural—turkey, chicken, dairy, fruit and hop farming—but by 1892 the town could boast an architect, veterinary surgeon and photography shop. Trains were running through Lacey four times daily and population had reached 500 by that year.

Industrial production began in Lacey when Union Mills was opened in 1910. Built at the tip of Long Lake, the mill, which was rebuilt in 1912, boasted the most modern of facilities which could cut 150,000 board feet of lumber a day. The mill had its own hotel, houses, company store, post office, and pool hall. With the decline in the supply of timber, the mill closed in the 1920s.

The Olympia Hotel built in 1889 fronted Main between Seventh and Eighth streets.

The grand Victorian structure was built of wood, four stories high and encircled by verandas.

It featured the latest in conveniences with both gas and electricity, central heating, a lobby, elevator, bar, laundry, and clubroom.

Built at a cost of $100,000 with $80,000 coming from the community, the hotel suffered some financial reversals but not before hosting many gala events. Gen. T. I. McKenny, T. M. Reed, Mrs. Pamela Hale, and Mrs. A. H. Stuart led the civic effort to build the hotel.

The structure burned in a spectacular fire in 1904. State Capital Museum photo

The Olympia Opera House was built in 1890 by newspaperman John Miller Murphy at a cost of $30,000. The towered structure was located at Fourth and Jefferson downtown. Designed under the direction of the Scientific American, *the theater had a 1000-seat capacity, art glass doors, maroon plush seats, electric lights, and oak and redwood on the interior.*

During the next thirty years, a variety of acts including John Philip Sousa, Mark Twain, the Barrymores, and minstrel shows played to large crowds. The theater met the wrecking ball in 1925 with the advent of movie houses. State Capital Museum photo

In 1893 the growth continued when the Catholic Benedictine Order founded St. Martin's College on part of Wood's original claim. The Order bought 470 acres through the good offices of A. H. Chambers, area pioneer and mayor of Olympia.

The Benedictine monks worked hard to erect the first building for their college in 1895—a mansard-roofed four-floor structure. The wooden buildings were replaced, beginning in 1913, with the present brick structures which were completed in the 1920s. Although the school opened with only one student in 1895, it has grown with Lacey to become an outstanding institution.

In Tumwater, too, events were transpiring which were to have a long-range effect. While contracting some business in Olympia, Leopold B. Schmidt, a German native and owner of a brewery in Butte, Montana, sampled the artesian wells in Tumwater. After analyzing the water professionally, he decided to move his brewery to Tumwater to take advantage of the remarkable water. Capital Brewing Company produced its first beer, Olympia Pale Export, in October 1896. At first housed in wooden buildings, Schmidt built his magnificent six-story brick Italianate brewhouse below the lower falls in 1906.

By the turn of the century the capital area was awash in bicycle mania and the old fairgrounds near what is now Carlyon Avenue which had been used as a baseball park were converted to a bicycle racing track (velodrome) during the years from 1900 to 1903. In 1903 the site again returned to use as a baseball park.

Out on the waterfront, activities were again under way to dredge the harbor when the Army Corps of Engineers dredged the channel in 1893-94 and deposited the dirt under the Fourth Street bridge. In usual civic booster style, city businessmen accepted warrants for the workmen. By 1895 the long wharf was abandoned as the dredging allowed more extensive use of Percival Dock built by the famed Percival family in 1891. By the turn of the century lumber trade was the mainstay of the port. Lumber ships loaded the products of area mills from scows. The Brenner family built an oyster export dock near the Deschutes Waterway.

The small community of Boston Harbor north of Olympia was the scene of much activity during the decade following the turn of the century. First planned as a new metropolis to be named Harriman City, Dofflemyer Point was chosen by promoter C. D. Hillman in 1907 as a major port. Promised were smelters, lumber mills, iron and steel works, and a harbor, all

The Tribune, *one of Olympia's numerous newspapers, published a souvenir edition in 1891. On the cover was this drawing by Edward Lange, a prominent artist who worked in Olympia and Long Island, New York. In the rendering, Lange captured the optimism of the nineties in Olympia. Included were a vision of a new capital, a grand railroad station, the mills of Tumwater and a view of the harbor. Schmidt House Collection photo*

served by a major railroad. But by 1911 Hillman was on trial for mail fraud and only a few buildings were started at Boston Harbor where hundreds had purchased lots.

In 1905 P. H. Carlyon was elected mayor of Olympia. The inveterate booster of Olympia produced promotion booklets, enacted an ordinance that only brick, stone, or concrete buildings be erected in the business district (perhaps because of the hotel fire) and tried to clean up the city's water supply. He also led the drive to purchase the former site of the Oblate Mission at Priest Point for a city park.

The decade wound up with a gala Legislative Ball in Tumwater when streetcar service for 600 was provided to the Tumwater Hall.

This shows early training for the National Guard of Washington Territory, Company A, First Regiment, circa the 1890s.

R. G. O'Brien, quartermaster-general of the Territory, organized the first guard in 1883. The first anniversary of the guard was celebrated by a masquerade in the Columbia Hall in 1884.

With statehood the guard was reorganized in 1891 when forty-five militiamen were sworn in as Company A of the First Regiment. Officers were C. S. Reinhart, Captain; Mark E. Reed, First Lieutenant; and Second Lieutenant W. J. Milroy. The company drilled every Monday evening, here in front of the Olympia Opera House.

Company A was part of the 1,200 guardsmen encamped at Woodland in 1894. State Capital Museum photo

The McKenny Building was constructed by General T. I. McKenny in 1891 at the southwest corner of Capitol Way and Fourth (now Goldberg's). The building was leased to the state from 1890 to 1901 and housed state departments. Governor John Rogers, Secretary of State Will D. Jenkins, the Land Commission, the Supreme Court, and the Law Library were all housed here until Thurston County sold the state its new courthouse also built in 1891. When the state offices were in the McKenny Block, the legislature was held in the Old Capitol on the present grounds.

Later known as the Kneeland Hotel, the building was torn down after it suffered extensive damage in the 1949 earthquake. State Capital Museum photo

The Episcopal Church was built in 1891 at Ninth and Washington. This was the first organized Episcopal church in Washington. Some services were held at Hudson's Bay, at Nisqually, but in 1853 (Rev.) John McCarthy began preaching to the small settlement of Olympia and began regular services in 1854. The first appointed missionary was (Rev.) D. Ellis Willes in 1860, who held services in the Masonic Temple until 1864 when a lot at Seventh and Main was purchased. The parish was organized that same year and met in a converted carpenter shop.

Among early members were Elisha Ferry, T. I. McKenny, A. H. Steele, and Samuel Percival.

In 1878 the church bought the Ninth and Washington property and built a rectory. C. N. Daniels designed the church, which was built through contributions of former parishes of (Rev.) Buck, then pastor. The beautiful rose window, nine feet in diameter, was a gift of the young women's club of the parish founded by Mrs. T. N. Ford. The window was made in England at a cost of $500. State Capital Museum photo

T. I. McKenny was born in Illinois. He fought in the Mexican and Civil Wars and was an attaché to several generals. He was brevetted Brigadier General and graduated from Physicians College in 1866. In 1867, he was named Superintendent of Indian Affairs for Washington Territory.

He spent the rest of his life in Olympia where he was active in real estate, in the school system, and was president of the State Hospital in Steilacoom for a time. State Capital Museum photo

Olympia Building and Loan was originally the Capital National Bank Building, constructed in 1890 by well-known banker C. J. Lord. The structure was just south of the McKenny block and is now the site of Olympia Federal Savings. Jeffers Studio "Old Olympia" Collection photo

Sylvester Park was part of the original plat of Olympia made by New Englander Edmund Sylvester for his new town in 1850. In early years the park was used much as the town common, as a pasturage for animals. In 1856, a blockhouse was built to house settlers during the Indian Uprising on the town square.

In 1861 the square played a part in keeping the county seat of Thurston County in Olympia. Challenged that year by Tumwater, who pledged land and materials for a county courthouse, Olympians countered by offering the town square as a building site. Olympia won in a county plebiscite, but later it was discovered that Sylvester had donated the town square to stay in perpetuity as a park for public use.

The courthouse was eventually built across the street from the square.

The town often gathered in the park for celebrations such as Fourth of July, Memorial Day, and May Queen fests.

The square was landscaped in 1893, probably to complement the new courthouse which was complete with a Victorian gazebo and fishpond.

The property was deeded to the state when the capitol was designated across the street. During those years it was known as Capitol Plaza and many dignitaries spoke to crowds that gathered in the park. William Jennings Bryan, Teddy Roosevelt, Taft, and Franklin Roosevelt were some of the more famous speakers there.

After the capitol moved to the present grounds, the park reverted to the name of its founder and it was used for circuses, baseball, and miniature golf. In 1950, a log cabin was built in the park for Olympia's Centennial observance.

In 1955 the property was again challenged when plans were made to build a parking garage on the site. But petitions were circulated and Sylvester's grant as a public space remained safe. In 1976 the present gazebo was built as a Bicentennial project of the Patrons for South Sound Cultural Activities and the park remains a pleasant gathering place for all segments of Olympia. Sylvester Park. State Capital Museum photo from the Jeffers Collection

The Olympia Light and Power powerhouse was built in 1905 at the lower falls of the Deschutes River.

The powerhouse was first built at the middle falls in 1890 and later moved to the lower falls. There, flumes from the upper falls group brought extra water power to the more than ninety-foot drop of the three falls. The stone powerhouse served Olympia and Tumwater with electric light and power as well as streetcar service. State Capital Museum photo

Inside the lower powerhouse, two 800-horsepower turbine wheels were directly connected to 500-kilowatt generators. Transmission lines carried the generated power across Puget Sound to where manufacturers used the wattage, replacing gasoline and steam production. Henderson House Museum photo

Hazard Stevens established the Elk Farm along the falls of the Deschutes River as an attraction for streetcar riders at the end of the line in Tumwater.

Stevens, son of first Territorial Governor Isaac Stevens, came west with his mother to join the governor in the small settlement of Olympia in 1854. He accompanied his father on parleys with the Indians, served in the Civil War, and held many government positions in Washington Territory. He returned east in 1874 but in 1890 was active in organizing the Olympia Light and Power Company.

The Elk Farm was at the upper falls of the Deschutes where the Falls Park is now located. State Capital Museum photo

The Tumwater station of the Olympia, Tumwater and Brighton Park Railway was located near the Deschutes Bridge crossing and is pictured here circa 1895. State Capital Museum photo

Bush Baker, motorman of the Olympia Streetcar #3, is shown here in the late 1890s. The streetcar system was four miles of standard gauge track running from the eastern limits of the city to the business center and then south through Olympia to Tumwater. Regular service was at fifteen-minute intervals. State Capital Museum photo

By the 1890s Olympia's population had grown enough to merit the building of elementary new schools. Three imposing, towered, brick structures were built for Washington, Garfield, and Lincoln Schools. All of similar design, they each cost $25,000 and had eight schoolrooms. Each was replaced in the 1920s with a new Mission Style Building. Pictured here is Washington School with its pupils. State Capital Museum photo

Lincoln School was one of the schools built in 1891. However, soon after its completion, the tower collapsed and had to be rebuilt. State Capital Museum photo

Mr. and Mrs. George Huggins are seen in front of the old Capitol with the Reed Block which housed the Olympian *in the background. State Captial Museum photo*

The Thurston County Courthouse was built in 1891 by architect Willis Ritchie in the Richardson Romanesque style then popular for public buildings. The octagonal clock tower, a great source of civic pride, burned in 1928 and had to be razed after the 1949 earthquake. The building was recently renovated as offices for the Superintendent of Public Instruction at a cost of $9 million. The building was home for state government from 1905 to 1928 and is listed on the National Register of Historic Places.

Fronting the old Capitol is a statue of Governor John Rogers who as a state legislator was father of the "Barefoot Schoolboy Law" which guaranteed funding for education statewide. Schoolchildren of Washington contributed to its erection in Sylvester Park. State Capital Museum photo from the Jeffers Collection

These were the mill workers, circa 1915.

Where the Weyerhaeuser plant now stands in Lacey, one of the first electric sawmills in the northwest once spewed out 120,000 board feet of lumber per day and employed hundreds of men. The Union Lumber Company and its small milltown of Union Mills are the legacy of many Laceyites.

The mill was owned by the Chattan family, associated with the Fletcher-Coward Company of Kansas City where the lumber was shipped for retail sale. First built in 1910, the mill burned and was reconstructed in 1912. Power was generated on-site with steam boilers and a steam turbine to power the facility which produced dimensional lumber, lath, and shingles. Specialties included the "tung-lock silo," a notched product for water towers and silos; tongue-in-groove ready-cut pieces for home building; and "jap-squares" which were logs squared and sold to Japan for shipment without further sawing.

Working twelve-hour days, the mill workers first logged around Patterson Lake and floated logs through a canal to Long Lake. Later, a railroad was built to Hogum Bay and logging commenced there and at South Bay. Three locomotives brought logs pulled from the woods by donkey engines over the railway. The railway bed is still visible near the mill site at Mesplay Road, which was named for a mill engineer. Later, logs came from Union Burn and Hanaford Valley at Bucoda. A trestle was built into Long Lake which dumped the logs for storage before milling. A tugboat maneuvered logs to the conveyor near the lake where logs were fed into the mill.

For married employees, the Union Mills Company built houses, many of which still stand on Union Mills Road. The homes of the general manager and superintendent still remain today.

The single working men lived in a three-story hotel opposite the mill. Here about seventy men roomed and were fed in a large dining hall. The building housed a store, post office, pool hall, and barbershop. The community often had dances, movies, dinners, and talent shows.

Another group of workers was the

Japanese, who lived separately east of the main mill. Supervised by English-speaking foremen, they worked on the "green chain" in the mill, separating sizes of lumber. The lumber was stacked by hand and left to air or kiln dry on the premises.

The mill closed in 1925 after a fire at its timber source in Bucoda. The cost of transporting logs to the mill also made further operations uneconomical. The mill was dismantled and the hotel eventually torn down in the 1930s.

In this montage, the railroad roundhouse is in the upper left and the shingle mill is at the upper right. The smokestack is from the generating plant, and the two houses (still standing today) are the superintendent's and the general manager's. The large building at right is the hotel, and below is the planing mill. The lake is at the left and a wide view of the mill is at the bottom left. Photograph courtesy of Roy and Pat Rossow

The Woodland Driving Park was organized by Isaac C. Ellis, a local logger. He had cleared several acres in Woodland (Lacey), and built a clubhouse, stables, and grandstand.

The track was 1,600 feet in length and was judged one of the best in the west. The track and two-story clubhouse were within thirty feet of the train depot. The clubhouse had a dining room, kitchen, parlors, and twelve rooms on the second floor. On either side of the clubhouse were two stables 500 feet long. The park formally opened May 25, 1891.

For many years the track drew large crowds and the elaborate clubhouse was later converted into the Lacey Hotel, first operated by the Kenney family and later by Mr. and Mrs. George Huggins. In July 1939 the old building was torn down. The barns and pasture were later used as a brood farm and practice track.

Lacey Downs shopping center was built at the site during the 1980s and the track has been marked by the Lacey Historical Society. Photo from "Olympia," an Olympia Chamber of Commerce publication, circa 1900

This is a photo of Tumwater looking westward circa 1907. On the far right is the S. N. Cooper Mill and glazing shop built in 1886. To the left is the Robert Esterly House with the McIntosh residence in the center with the fenced yard. The Henderson House (now the Tumwater Museum), built in 1905, is to the left of the brewery building in the background.

In the foreground of the photo is the brewery wharf to the right; bottling plant, streetcar, which was used for freight and passenger transportation; and bottling plant.

The tall building to the left is the first brewhouse and storage plant built in 1906. State Capital Museum photo

Main Street (now Capitol Way) was photographed looking north in about 1895. The Woodruff Block is on the right as are the Mottman Building and the McKenny Block. The Chambers Block with its decorative cornice is on the left. State Capital Museum photo

This was the interior of the I. Harris Drygoods Store, later sold to Millers Department Store.

Isaac Harris came to Olympia in 1870 and operated his first store in the Tilley Block at Third and Main. His son Mitchel Harris continued the business for many years at 510 Main, and was twice elected mayor of Olympia. State Capital Museum photo

This was Olympia looking east from Water Street with the Olympia Hotel to the far right and the Courthouse—old Capitol to the left of center and magnificent Mt. Rainier in the background. Schmidt House Photo Collection

This was a view of Olympia about 1900 looking northeast with the Providence Academy to the left front and Olympia Hotel to the left rear. Also seen are the city hall (Columbia Hall) to the right of the hotel and the Masonic temple on Capitol Way to the far right of the hotel. Photo by A. D. Rogers from the State Capital Museum Collection

er the state purchase of the grand
ered and turreted Thurston
nty Courthouse, this more
dest structure was built in 1900 a
corner of Fourth and Washington
he northeast corner next to the
Columbia Hall.
he courthouse was constructed o
ino sandstone shipped to Olym-
over the old Port Townsend-
thern railroad to the west side
ot and brought by horse and
g to the site.
harles Patnude, an Olympia con-
tor, built the building, which was
d in 1934. State Capital Museum
to

At the turn of the century cycling was the rage and Olympians were no exception to the trend. A bicycle racing track (velodrome) was constructed in 1899 at the fairgrounds in Tumwater, then transformed into a racetrack in 1906, and still later became the Carlyon Addition. State Capital Museum photo

These were local cycling enthusiasts. State Capital Museum photo

At the end of the Spanish-American War in 1902, a ceremonial procession was held down Main Street to the Masonic Cemetery in Tumwater. At the end of the march a burial ceremony was held for an unknown soldier killed in the Philippines. Here onlookers greet the cortege in front of the Olympia Hotel. State Capital Museum photo

The streets of Olympia, the Hotel Olympia, and a cable car were bedecked with bunting for a Fourth of July celebration. Schmidt House Photo Collection

In the days before university locations had been established by the legislature, Olympia was the gathering place for a number of educational institutions.

Under the auspices of the Methodist Episcopal Church, the first college was organized in 1858 as the Puget Sound Wesleyan Institute and was housed at Washington and Union streets. In 1861 it was reorganized as the Olympia Union Academy and in 1869 a new building, pictured here, was built at Olympia Street and East Bay Drive near the Daniel Bigelow home. Bigelow, a prominent educator and lawyer, had been a driving force in organizing the college. Renamed the Olympia Collegiate Institute in 1883, the school educated a number of citizens under a normal program until 1893 when a depression and interest in moving the facility to Tacoma forced its closure. The dormitory had just been added in 1890.

The building was used by J. R. Chaplin and later by the Pacific Lutheran Evangelical Seminary and Olympia public schools. The building was torn down in the 1920s. State Capital Museum photo

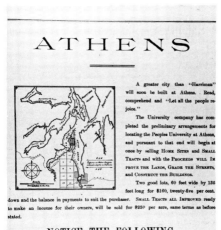

In 1891 a Congregationalist minister, J. R. Chaplin, platted College Grove on Cooper Point for his Olympic University. Those plans did not materialize but in 1900 he again platted a community called "Athens" on Cooper Point under the aegis of the University Company. "The People's University," a stock-supported institution with such progressive ideas as part-time courses for working people and traveling universities, was his plan. By 1906 People's University had moved into temporary quarters in the OCI building but the institution never reached Cooper Point, where the plat of Athens was abandoned in 1914.

Some land was cleared and trees were planted which still remain on the site, along with some names in remembrance of the utopian plan. State Capital Museum photo

St. Martin's College opened its doors in September 1895. The Benedictine Order had sought out a location in western Washington for a monastery and college. In early 1893, they chose a site at Dryad near Centralia.

However, Father Charles Classens, pastor of Olympia, persuaded the Benedictines to extend their search to the Olympia area and with the help of local businessman A. H. Chambers, they located a section of land near what was then Woodland. The area offered a panoramic hilltop covered with virgin timber which attracted the priests. Not only that, but the spot conveniently adjoined the Northern Pacific Railway.

More than $1,600 was raised with the help of Chambers and Olympia Mayor John Byrnes, for the purchase of land in 1894.

By September 1895, the dense timber had been cleared and the hilltop boasted a four-story brick and wooden structure featuring a mansard roof and landmark bell tower. Opening day that September had

only one student, but the college has endured and grown throughout its long history in Lacey. Lacey Museum photo

Early buildings at St. Martin's included, at far left, the Music House, originally built for the brothers and workmen in 1906; the Infirmary built in 1911, at center; and the shoe shop, carpenter, and blacksmith shop, to the right, which was the first hilltop building and later moved. Lacey Museum photo

Workers from the Lea Lumber shingle mill in Tumwater posed in front of the mill in 1904. Henderson House Museum photo

Boston Harbor north of Olympia has been settled since 1865 when the Dofflemyer family made a land claim from the point southward.

In 1904 a newspaperman and lawyer, P. P. Carroll, announced plans for a seaport at Dofflemyer Point to be named Harriman City, after the president of the Southern Pacific and Union Pacific railways who had promised, said Carroll, to extend his lines to a new terminus at Harriman City.

This was all magic to the rail-starved citizens of Olympia, but when he expected them to buy $20,000 worth of stock, their enthusiasm waned.

In 1907 another promoter, C. D. Hillman, fresh from creating over fifteen new towns and additions around Seattle, set his eyes on Dofflemyer Point.

Hillman started building on the pilings left by Carroll and started a media blitz by distributing a graphic pamphlet which illustrated in detail what his new city, Boston Harbor, was going to be like. Huge ships filled the harbor while shipyards, mills, and smelters clogged the paper waterfront. Impressive homes and the happy people who inhabited them were pictured as well.

Excursions from Tacoma, Seattle, and Olympia brought droves of buyers who bought over 2,000 lots in one day.

Hillman did purchase 5,000 acres of land and some buildings were started at the town site and water pipes laid. But in 1911 Hillman was on trial on thirteen counts of mail fraud and the promotion fell by the wayside.

In the late 1920s yet another plan for Boston Harbor was unveiled. Olympia Homes, under the ownership of Carlton Sears, purchased 1,600 lots and five miles of waterfront for development, but the depression cancelled these plans.

In 1935, Governor Clarence Martin proposed a federal rural rehabilitation project for Boston Harbor to create an industrial community with a plywood factory on Zangle Cove, but this, too, came to naught.

The area is now occupied by summer and permanent homes and a marina. Illustration from a booklet in the collection of Ted and Pauline Robinson

Camping scene on our water front 5 acre tracts at Boston Harbor. Eight Fresh Water Lakes full of trout and black bass, fine clam and oyster beds.

Grass 8 foot high grows here, fine for Dairying, no winter feeding

Over $600 in berries raised on one acre at Boston Harbor

Eggs 25 to 65 cents a dozen all year at Seattle or Everett. A lady at Boston Harbor makes $250 per month raising chickens and Belgian hares.

C. D. HILLMAN
the largest land owner in the State of Washington

Boston Harbor

The place that will make thousands of happy and prosperous homes.

We build this house for $525 on terms of $25 down $10 per month. Why do some people pay rent?

One of C. D. Hillman's promotions of his new metropolis at Boston Harbor.

Hillman placed full-page ads in area papers promising "Free Excursion Tomorrow. Big clam bake and barbecue on the beautiful grounds on Boston Harbor. Two orchards of ripe fruit thrown open to the public. A band will furnish music."

Who could resist a free ride on a big paddlewheel steamboat on a Sunday afternoon? On one October Sunday in 1907, more than 2,000 people were on the grounds at Boston Harbor. From Olympia came the Multnomah loaded with passengers. From Seattle, the steamer Yosemite brought 1,700 people, which nearly exceeded its load limit.

So popular was the trip that the steamer had to leave 500 waiting at the dock in Seattle. An estimated $100,000 in sales were made during the trip before the steamer even docked at Boston Harbor!

One of the overloaded steamers is seen docking at the wharf here in 1907. State Capital Museum photo

The Priest Point Park Pavilion was built in 1905. Leopold Schmidt donated the structure which had been the Olympia Brewery building at the Portland Lewis & Clark 1904 Exposition. It was rebuilt by volunteers at the park.

The former location of the Oblate Catholic Mission in 1848, the park area in the early 1900s fell into the hands of developers who were experiencing financial difficulties. When the parklands reverted to the county for delinquent taxes, the city opted to buy 240 acres for a park.

The landscaping work was done by citizens who joined in clambakes and other activites while working on the park. The pavilion was the crowning touch to this effort. State Capital Museum photo

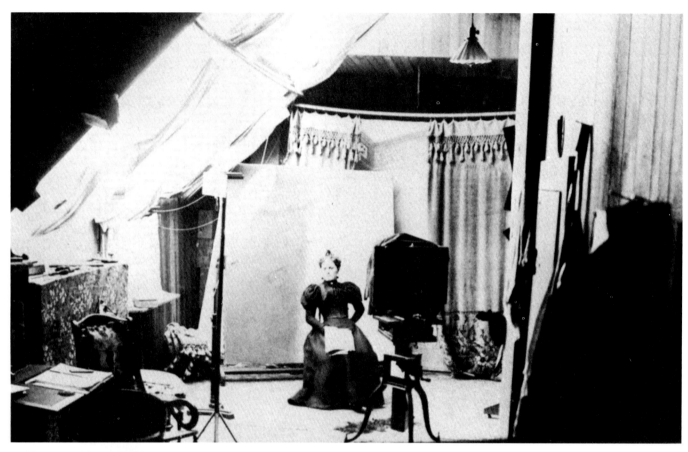

Ida B. Smith posed in her photography studio at 523 Main Street about 1895.

Mrs. Smith, who lived from 1851 to 1923, had a photography business for a number of years around the turn of the century. Notice the north light window, so necessary before the days of sophisticated electrical lighting. State Capital Museum photo

The interior of A. D. Rogers Photography Studio at 502 Main Street in Olympia circa 1906 is shown. State Capital Museum photo

Traffic and a streetscape on North Fourth Street looking east are shown in this 1906 view. To the left is the Mottman Building and to the right the McKenny Block. The towered structure in the background is the Columbia City Hall building. State Capital Museum photo

Street activity on Fourth Street looking west was captured in this 1909 photograph. State Capital Museum photo

Abbie Howard Hunt Stuart was known as the "Mother of Northwest Women's Clubs" and was the founder and first president of the Olympia group.

Mrs. Stuart's husband was U.S. Land Office Receiver in Olympia and Mrs. Stuart took over his work after his death in 1902. She was also an active member of the suffrage movement for women in Washington and a number of other civic organizations. State Capital Museum photo

The Women's Clubhouse was built in 1906 at 1002 S. Washington.

Founded in 1883, one of the oldest women-only clubs on the West Coast, the Women's Club first met in the Sylvester House. From teaching domestic arts, the club branched out to discussions of papers dealing with local and national political and social questions.

The club has taken the lead in many civic and philanthropic concerns during its more than 100 years of history, including maintenance of the library for Olympia during the years of 1896-1909.

The unique clubhouse was designed to blend in with the surrounding residential architecture. The building has been placed on the National Register of Historic Places. State Capital Museum photo

Paving crews brought a metropolitan air to Olympia as they moved along West Fourth here in about 1909. State Capital Museum photo

William Winlock Miller High School, built in 1907, was on Columbia between 13th and 14th. Built at a cost of $26,845 in Tenino sandstone, the stucture was sold to the state with the expansion of the capitol grounds. The building burned in 1918.

William Winlock Miller came to Olympia in 1853 from Illinois. He was a businessman who volunteered for the militia in the 1885-86 uprising and was named commissary general and staff officer to Isaac Stevens, with whom he became a close friend. Miller was later named Superintendent of Indian Affairs.

His family donated land for the first high school and each succeeding building has been named in his honor. State Capital Museum photo

In 1909 George Funk and his sister Mrs. Addie Volland built this building at the corner of Fifth and Main in Olympia. George Funk and his wife Goldie Robertson Funk were both prominent in Olympia affairs. Mrs. Funk was a writer and member of the Women's Club. Her husband was an attorney who had offices in this building. He brought suit to insist that state government offices be located in Olympia thus ensuring prominence for the capital city. "Old Olympia" photo from the Jeffers Studio Collection

The Olympia Knitting Mills Company, headquartered on Jefferson between Fifth and Sixth streets, was organized in 1909 by George Mottman, C. H. Springer, and Mitchell Harris. Later the Whiting, Ingham, and Lord families became proprietors of the operation.

The mills made college sweaters, bathing suits, and dresses. The concern closed in 1939. State Capital Museum photo

Shown are some of the workers inside the mill. State Capital Museum photo

Here is a closer view of the machines used in the knitting of clothes. State Capital Museum photo

Mollie Moore was queen of the Women's Club float along with a bevy of young women representing the states of the union on this Fourth of July exhibition. The float is passing by the Caledonia Hotel which stood on the north side of Fifth Street between Main (Capitol Way) and Washington. Circa 1910. State Capital Museum Photo

The Tumwater Club was formed in 1908 by Brewery employees and the building was built as a Bachelor's Club for them by Peter and Adolph Schmidt. A number of social events were held here including inaugural balls and it later housed a roller rink. The building which was located at 3300 S. Capitol Way burned in December 1955. Henderson House photo

The interior of the grand ballroom of the Tumwater Club is shown here gaily decorated. Henderson House Museum photo

Crowds gathered to witness a balloon ascent south of Capital Way here in 1910. The balloon was sponsored by the Singer Sewing Machine Company. State Capital Museum photo

Steamers in Olympia circa 1911 are, at left, the Venus *at Horr's Dock, and, at right, the* S. G. Simpson *at Percival. The* Venus *was built at Friday Harbor in 1907, used for Puget Sound excursions, and burned in 1915. State Capital Museum photo*

Steamboat Travel

As one of the first major settlements on Puget Sound and the Territorial Capital, Olympia was an early destination in the steamboat traffic that plied Puget Sound.

The British settlement at Nisqually in 1831 brought the first resident vessel, the *Beaver*, to the sound in 1836, although British, Spanish, and American ships had explored the waters of Puget Sound, and Native Americans had traveled these inland waters in their swift canoes for hundreds of years.

The *Orbit* from San Francisco was the first ship to call at Olympia on January 1, 1850 where it loaded pilings for San Francisco.

The first Puget Sound Collection District and Custom House was establsihed at Olympia in 1851. The first coasting license was issued to the *George Emery* in November of that year. Olympia lost the Custom House to Port Townsend in 1854.

By 1851, a brisk trade in lumber was operating between Olympia and San Francisco. The ships also took on coal, shingles and salmon. In 1852, for example, the brig *June* loaded 800 piles, 2000 barrels of salmon, 140,000 shingles and thirty cords of wood.

In 1853 Edmund Sylvester built a scow *Schictwoo* and the *G. W. Kendall* called at Olympia bringing a hug cargo of merchandise to start a store.

The steamship era began in 1853 with the arrival c the small side-wheel steamer *Fairy* in Olympia on boar the bark *Sarah Warren*. However, the timber trad continued to be the primary traffic.

The steamers were the most picturesque of th ships on the sound and their arrival at any port was cause for civic celebration. The best source of news unt the advent of the telegraph in 1864, the steamer brought the outside world to the small settlement around Puget Sound.

To attract more of the steamers, Edward Gidding built a long wharf in 1854 extending from the foot of Mair Street in Olympia. The Victoria to Olympia (capital tc capital) mail run was a lucrative contract which wa taken by the *Emilie Parker,* the *Traveler,* and the *Majo Tompkins.*

Steamboat traffic stepped up in 1857 when Captair A. B. Rabbeson ran the small *Fairy* between Steilacoom and Olympia. The Fraser River gold rush in 1858 brought bigger side-wheelers like the *Constitution* anc

This drawing of Olympia's West Side Mills shows traffic with early steamers and sailing ships. From the Schmidt House Collection

Wilson G. Hunt to Puget Sound. Under a $36,000 yearly contract, the Eliza Anderson, one of the most renowned of the early steamers, was running on the Victoria to Olympia route.

Samuel Percival built a waterfront dock in 1860 and renovated it in 1865. The government survey brig Fauntleroy mapped Puget Sound in 1866 setting the stage for government dredging of Olympia's mud-bound harbor.

A number of vessels were built in Olympia and in 1871 the Puget Sound Steam Navigation Company was incorporated there.

The need for a new wharf was brought to the fore when Captain J. G. Parker in 1875 solicited Goodall, Nelson & Perkins to locate a steamship terminus in Olympia on the condition a new wharf would be built. Brown's Wharf, now known as "Old Port," brought the terminus. Unfortunately, the wood-destroying worm teredo made short work of the pilings, so despite rail access to the dock, the facility received limited use.

A long wharf to deep water was again extended from Main, 4798 feet long in 1885 and the big steamers T. J. Potter and Emma Hayward, owned by the Oregon Railway and Navigation Company returned to Olympia and in 1891 Percival constructed a new dock along Water Street. By 1895 the long wharf was abandoned as dredging allowed for extensive use of Percival Dock. The S. Willey Navigation Company brought the steamers Multnomah, City of Aberdeen and Capital City on South Sound runs.

The filling and dredging of the harbor brought a final flurry of steamboat activity after the turn of the century to Olympia docks when the Nisqually, piloted by Capt. Volney Young, joined the steamers Greyhound, Multnomah and Capital City of the Olympia-Tacoma Navigation Company, organized in 1903.

By the 1920s local steamboating had almost entirely given way to the advent of the more convenient highways for intra-sound transportation and the glorious days of the steamers were gone.

The T. J. Potter, one of the famous Puget Sound steamers, was built in Portland in 1888. Measuring 230 feet long with a 35-foot beam and 10½-foot draft, the ship was on the Olympia-Tacoma Seattle run. In 1892, it was transferred, as were many of the sound steamers, to the Columbia River, and in 1925 broke up at Astoria. Washington State Library photo

John C. Percival stands proudly in front of his Percival Landing office. Percival, who had been given charge of the dock in 1877 at age sixteen, had one of the most remarkable careers imaginable in the steamboat era. From 1877 to 1936 he was agent for Goodall, Perkins & Company and its successors, Pacific Coast Steamship Line, Pacific Steamships, the Admiral Line as well as Oregon Railway and Navigation Co., and Northern Pacific. Jeffers photo from the Schmidt House Collection

The S.S. Willie ran between Olympia and Shelton from 1886 to 1900. The craft was owned and operated by Lan and Lafe Willey, sons of Sam Willey, early settler and logger. Here it has put in at Percival's Dock. Photo courtesy of Gordon Newell

The Northern Light, City of Shelton, and Multnomah of the S. Willey Navigation Company are shown here after the deepening of Percival Dock. State Capital Museum photo

The Bailey Gatzert *was a legend in Puget Sound for its speed. Launched in 1890 in Seattle by the Seattle Steam Navigation & Transportation Company, the vessel measured 177 feet long by 32 feet of beam and 8 feet of draft. Later owned by the Columbia River and Puget Sound Transportation Company, the boat was used as an auto ferry on the Seattle-Bremerton run beginning in 1918 and was dismantled in 1926. Photo courtesy of Gordon Newell*

The Capital City, *part of the S. Willey Steam Navigation Company, was built in 1898 at Port Blakely. It was first named the* Dalton. *The ship was used on the Olympia-Tacoma route and for excursions. Photo courtesy of Gordon Newell*

The City of Shelton *was built at Shelton in 1895 and was used on the Olympia-Shelton Route to succeed the* Willie *and used as a spare boat after the S. G. Simpson. After 1912 the ship was sold to the American Tug Boat Company and broke up in the Deadwater Slough in 1930. Photo courtesy of Gordon Newell*

Launched by Crawford and Reid at Tacoma in 1907, the S. G. Simpson *was owned by Mark Reed and used on the Shelton-Olympia-Tacoma route. The boat later was on the Portland-Astoria Columbia River run. Photo courtesy Gordon Newell*

The Greyhound *was built in 1889, measuring 140 feet long and 18 feet wide at midships. The ship was brought to the sound in 1892 for the Olympic-Tacoma Navigation Company on that run and nearly sank at Percival Dock in 1904. The steamer charged fifty cents to Tacoma and was a competitor to the* Multnomah. *Photo courtesy of Gordon Newell*

The Yosemite was built in 1865 by the California Steam & Navigation Company. Rebuilt in 1883 for the Canadian Pacific, after a boiler explosion, the steamer was again refitted in 1906 at Bainbridge Island for excursions all over Puget Sound including Brewery excursions to Olympia. Photo courtesy of Gordon Newell

Nisqually was a twentieth-century steamboat built at Dockton. It measured 140 feet long and 23 feet wide, with a sharp hull. In 1911 it was put on the Olympia-Tacoma-Seattle run replacing the Greyhound. The ship was renamed the Astorian on the Columbia River service in 1918 and was sunk at Seattle in 1923. State Capital Museum photo

The Governor Elisha Ferry *was a State Fisheries cruiser based at Olympia beginning in 1914. Photo courtesy of Gordon Newell*

The small steamer City of Olympia *was built in 1898 for the Alaskan goldrush and was sent to Skagway. Here it is shown at Percival Dock. Photo courtesy of Gordon Newell*

Firemen displayed their first motorized fire truck here in about 1902. Shown are driver Claude Barnes, Chief Ed Raymond; on the far side of the truck, Elton Conant; on the running board, Assistant Chief Burt Barnes; leaning against the engine, Ed Scully; and riding the end, Charles Lincoln. State Capital Museum photo

1910-1930

The new decade began propitiously with continued dredging and filling of Olympia's harbor. During the years 1909-1911 the dredging filled much of what is now north downtown Olympia and part of the Deschutes Waterway. Known as the Carlyon Fill after its organizer and promoter, P. H. Carlyon, the dredging changed the shape of Olympia by adding some twenty-nine blocks of land in an effort which removed two million cubic yards of mud. Much of the land north of Olympia Avenue is fill. The cost was $250,000 and with a civic effort all but $58,000 was paid for by townspeople. Carlyon also persuaded railroad concerns to extend beltlines on the fill to serve the prospering mill industries.

Increased building accompanied the work on the port area. A new city hall, Masonic temple, federal building, and a third story on Mottman's Mercantile were built.

Plans for a new Capitol Group were finalized and the Temple of Justice on the capitol grounds got underway. Some old institutions disappeared when the Gold Bar Restaurant, site of the first territorial legislative assembly was torn down in 1911 and marked by a plaque on Capitol Way. John Miller Murphy, long-time newspaperman, died in 1915 and his glorious Olympia Theater was torn down in 1920. Another former legislative meeting place, the Farquhar Store, was also razed that year and the Stevens Mansion on the capitol grounds fell to the wrecker in 1929.

Prohibition closed down the brewery in Tumwater when Washington voted dry in 1914. When national prohibition came into effect, the Tumwater plant began producing "Appleju," an apple drink. By 1921, however, the unsuccessful venture closed its doors.

The Capital Community was involved as was all America in World War I. Olympia shipbuilding commenced in 1917 when the Olympia Ship Building Company constructed three five-masted schooners for Norwegian owners. Later the Sloan Shipyard took over the site and at the height of its activity had fourteen active ways at Olympia and Anacortes. Residents bought Liberty Bonds, knitted gloves and provided entertainment for nearby Fort Lewis soldiers.

Another rush of building activity took place after the war when the new Elks Building, Hotel Olympia and American Legion Hall were built all clustered near Sylvester Park in downtown Olympia. They were joined by the new Capital National Bank building and the Olympia Veneer Company on the port fill, the new

Dredging of the Olympia harbor got under way in earnest in 1910. The Carlyon fill added twenty-nine blocks to downtown Olympia and additional dredging in the 1920s set the stage for development of the Port of Olympia.

Lincoln School, the new St. Peter's Hospital and in 1924 the Capitol and Liberty Theaters.

Thurston County voters approved the creation of a Port District in 1922, in part to serve the extensive output of area mills which were rafting over 500 million board feet of lumber down the sound for shipment. The port built timber docks, piling and tracks throughout the 1920s culminating in the record-breaking cargo years of 1928 to 1930 when the port hosted hundreds of ships and shipped out over 298 million board feet of lumber.

The Olympia Yacht Club first organized in 1889 as the Olympia Motor Boat Club; it was reactivated in 1908 and by 1915 it had moorings at the city dock and in 1930 opened its first clubhouse.

Radio station KGY began broadcasting under an

official license in 1922. The station begun by Father Sebastian Ruth, a St. Martin's monk, was one of the first in the nation. Fr. Sebastian first began broadcasting from St. Martin's in Lacey in 1914 from a telegraph station and in the summer of 1921 began experiments in voice transmission. By January 1922 listeners could look forward to regular programs on Sunday, Tuesday and Friday evenings—a schedule which lasted through the eleven years of KGY's residence at St. Martin's. Ruth brought a wide array of programming including operas, live performances, and conducted a radio telegraph school of the air. The station became a commercial concern and moved from St. Martin's in 1932 to a downtown Olympia location.

St. Martin's began constructing their new brick buildings in 1913 and completed them in 1923. Gone were the Victorian wooden structures of the 1890s.

In the 1920s when travel was made easier through the use of automobiles, Lacey became a favorite vacation spot as resorts sprang up around the lakes. The resorts featured picnicking, swimming slides, water wheels, boats, fishing, dance halls, skating rinks and rental cabins. Seven resorts were located around Hicks Lake alone.

In 1927 the magnificent Legislative Building, the centerpiece of the Capitol Group, was completed—the final resting place of the capital was assured in Olympia.

Inspired by the flight of Charles Lindbergh across the Atlantic in 1927, Olympians became interested in the air age. Back in 1911 Olympians had seen their first air show and from that time until the late 1920s various visiting aircraft entertained as a novelty. Local barnstormers began to use the prairies south of Tumwater as a landing spot and the Chamber of Commerce of Olympia purchased the prairie to insure Olympia's place in aviation history. The city passed a bond issue in late 1928 to buy the airport property.

The airport installed a beacon which in those days was the only aid to night flying. A beacon was also planned atop the capitol dome.

While progress continued elsewhere with the building of the new Montgomery Ward store and the Washington Veneer plant on the port fill, the clock tower on the old capitol suffered a fire in 1928 and the old picturesque bandstand in the park adjoining it was torn down.

P. H. "Doc" Carlyon was trained as a dentist in Philadelphia and came to Olympia in 1884 to practice dentistry. Elected mayor in 1904, he embarked on his career as a booster of Olympia. In 1907 he was elected to the state legislature where he served until 1929.

Besides organizing the fill effort, Carlyon solicited rail lines to the port area, promoted the building of permanent capitol grounds, the building of Capitol Lake and supported the paving of roads statewide. State Capital Museum photo

This is part of a page from a promotional booklet initiated by P. H. Carlyon, describing Olympia as the land of opportunity. From the State Capital Museum Collection

The Jeffers Studio was built in 1913 by Joseph Wohleb for pioneer photographer Joseph Jeffers. The studio had the north light window and stucco style which was to become Wohleb's trademark in his long tenure as Olympia's foremost architect.

The Reed home is in the background. "Old Olympia" photo from the Jeffers Studio Collection

Under the auspices of the local Chamber of Commerce, Fred J. Wiseman brought a Curtiss Farman Wright plane to Olympia in May 1911. The "birdman," as the early fliers were called, took off and landed five times, each time for a three-minute duration. Motion pictures were taken which served to advertise the new fill which was ready for development. State Capital Museum photo

Onlookers watched the "birdman" fly over the fill in 1911.

The fill was a two-million-cubic-yard effort and much of the land north of Olympia Avenue is fill. The project cost $250,000 and all but $58,000 was paid for by the townspeople. State Capital Museum photo

The building which housed the firehouse and city hall was constructed in 1912 and used for both purposes until 1966, when the present city hall was built.

Olympia was first in the state to form a fire department, and the building has been placed on the State Register of Historic Places.

The building was the site of a stage station from Cowlitz Landing early in its history and later was the location of a livery stable. State Capital Museum photo

Firemen pictured in front of the old fire station are Grant Talcott, John Stewart, Alex Wright, William Weller, Joseph McCarragher, William Henry, Ausher Craig, and Sam McClelland.

The Alert Hook and Ladder Company was formed in Olympia in 1859 as a firefighting group. In 1865 the first Olympia volunteer group was organized and purchased a hand-pumping fire engine for $900. The engine was called the "Columbia," and the city hall built in 1869 was named for the engine, which was the pride and joy of the city. Other volunteer groups were the Squilgees and Olympia No. 1. In 1882 a major fire burned the block downtown bounded by Fourth, Fifth, Washington, and Main. This prompted the purchase of a horse-drawn Silsby steam pumper and the official organization of the fire fighting clubs in 1883 under the leadership of Joseph McCarragher as fire engineer.

In 1889 the Silsby was sent to Seattle on the steamer Fleetwood to help fight the major fire downtown. In fact, Seattleites showed their appreciation for this act by supporting Olympia for state capital when statehood was imminent.

In 1898 three more salaried firemen were hired and in 1902 Fire Chief Raymond combined all of the volunteers into one organization. State Capital Museum photo

The crew of the old Columbia posed in front of their beloved engine in 1888. Upper row: John McClellan; S. B. Henry; William Craig; George Allen, chief; Charles Talcott; Ed Robbins; and Joe Chilberg. Lower row: Clem Johnston, William Schofield, Joe Rizbeck, John Miller Murphy, Sam McClellan, Robert Frost, Dick Wood, and Ed Young. Schmidt House Collection photo

The Carlyon Fair Grounds in the Carlyon Addition area is shown circa 1911. Fred Carlyon, a brother to P. C. Carlyon, had developed a racetrack for harness races, pacers, and trotters at the site of the former velodrome. Traveling carnivals and the county fair were also located here. The site was especially popular because the trolley lines ran out to the area.

In the 1920s, Fred Carlyon graded the old fairgrounds site and began selling lots and naming the streets along this Carlyon Avenue for his family and friends. In all, he built twenty-eight homes in this area. Carlyon built himself a large home in 1908 where the Sunset Life building now stands. It was torn down after his death in 1956. Carlyon also developed the Carlyon Beach area near Olympia.
Henderson House Museum photo

Wilbur Ashley conducted a bicycle repair and motorcycle sales office near the end of the Tumwater bridge close to the Hewitt drugstore during the early years of the century. Mr. Ashley later had an auto equipment business near Percival Dock.
Henderson House Museum photo

A goldfish pond and Victorian bandstand were fixtures in Sylvester Park circa 1915 when Olympians gathered there for concerts and celebrations. Photo courtesy of Catherine Weller

The second William Winlock Miller High School was built in 1919 across the street from the Capitol Campus. It was designed, with the assistance of Tacoma architects Heath & Gove, by Joseph Wohleb. Because the former school had burned, all new furnishings were installed including a Talcott clock for $1,300, library books for $800, and $1,500 worth of new furniture.

The school was torn down in 1960 when the Capitol Campus expanded to east of Capitol Way. State Capital Museum photo

General Hazard Stevens, son of the first territorial governor Isaac Stevens, established Cloverfields Farm in 1914. The dairy sat on 260 acres, part of a claim purchased by Governor Isaac Stevens in 1853.

Stevens had come as a child of twelve to Olympia and accompanied the governor in parleys with the Indians. He later served in the Civil War where he was brevetted brigadier general and awarded the Medal of Honor. After the war he served in many capacities in Washington, such as collector of Internal Revenue and commissioner to settle land claims in the San Juan Islands. He read law with Elwood Evans in Olympia, and was active in helping the Olympia Railroad Union as well.

He returned in 1874 to his native Boston, and lived there until 1914 when his mother died and he came back to Olympia to found a model dairy farm called "Cloverfields."

He developed his father's claim which extended from Capitol Way to Cain Road. As the head of Olympia Light & Power Company, he promoted the use of electricity in his dairy, which boasted an all-electric barn and milking machines. In addition, the dairy was served by the latest in equipment, including galvanized steel fixtures, concrete floors, and separate sterilizing and bottling facilities. Water was piped from an artesian well which is still used by Olympia High School.

In 1917 Cloverfields milk was delivered for twelve cents a quart in modern delivery trucks. The Holstein dairy cattle were fed a scientifically formulated diet and tested for tuberculosis—both farsighted practices for the day.

By 1926 Cloverfields was offering milk from both Jerseys and Holsteins and receiving accolades from all fields of agriculture.

As the crowning touch to the farm, Hazard Stevens commissioned Joseph Wohleb to design a farmhouse to complement the farm. The Dutch Colonial farmhouse, at 1100 Carlyon Avenue, is on the National Register of Historic Places. State Capital Museum photo

This was a Cloverfields brochure. Courtesy of Helen Eskridge Rodman

This was the entry to Cloverfields Farm, where Carlyon Avenue now meets Capitol Way.

In its day the dairy and farmhouse presented an imposing and picturesque sight set overlooking a small lake named, appropriately, Lake Hazard. Holsteins grazed and Angora goats kept the lawns about the farmhouse closely cropped.

Stevens died in 1918 in Goldendale, but his farm and dairy continued for many years under the stewardship of Kate Stevens Bates, his sister.

During the 1930s the farm was divided into housing parcels of the Mt. View Addition and Stratford Place. The barns and outbuildings were torn down in 1949 and Olympia High School was built on the site.

Streets in the area of the original farm bear the names of the family and farm.

The Stevens House has been placed on the National Register of Historic Places. Photo courtesy of Helen Eskridge Rodman

The Georgian revival Olympian Hotel at the corner of Sixth and Washington was a worthy successor to the grand Olympian, and was the latest in a long line of hostelries designed to keep visiting legislators comfortable. Financed by locals, the hotel was designed by Stevens Company of Chicago and featured a grand ballroom and elegant appointments.

The opening of the hotel in June 1920 coincided with the opening of the Elks' new lodge, also facing the park, and the evening of their openings was one of Olympia's most memorable. The hotel was a favorite spot of legislators who until 1928 conducted business at the old Capitol, and it is said that more legislation was enacted in the Olympian than across the street during the heyday of the hotel.

The building has been renovated to accommodate senior citizen housing, and a number of shops occupy the first floor of the structure. The ballroom is still a favorite gathering spot of Olympians. Photo by Jeffers, courtesy of Kathy Engle

In 1915 the old David Chambers homestead and house was made into the Mt. View Golf Course just east of Lacey. The farmhouse was used as the clubhouse until 1961 when the area was redeveloped into Panorama City and the clubhouse used as a construction office. Some mementos of the house and Chambers family are still located in the Chalet at Panorama City. Lacey Museum photo

Lady golfers enjoy the links at the Mt. View Golf Course, circa 1920. Lacey Museum photo

Established in 1917 by E. R. Ward, the Ward Shipyards built three large five-masted schooners, 265 feet long and 48 feet of beam, for Norwegian owners. The ships were launched in 1917 and 1918, and in 1918 the property was acquired by Sloan Shipyard which developed a ten-way yard in Olympia. Henderson House Museum photo

The Olympia oyster has been an integral part of area culture since Native Americans first began to inhabit the coves and inlets of lower Puget Sound gathering this succulent shellfish. The ostrea lurida is found all over lower Puget Sound in Eld, Totten, Skookum, Hammersley, and South Bay inlets.

As early as 1853 settlers began appreciating the qualities of the oyster and a pioneer saying was, "When the tide is out, the table it set." Oysters and clams were lifesavers when other foods were in short supply.

Indians often sold oysters to settlers and by 1868 a brisk trade with San Francisco in Olympia oysters was under way. "Olympia, the home of the gods; Olympia oyster, food of the gods," was the motto.

With the coming of statehood in 1889 provisions were made under the Callow Act to enable the purchase of tidelands for oyster production. The native population was augmented through oyster cultivation beginning about 1890 when oyster boats and rafts for harvesting and washing were instituted.

During the drive to locate the capital in Olympia, oystermen sent their products to eastern Washington, and the oyster became known as the "succulent lobbyist" in acquiring votes for Olympia.

Doane's Oyster House, begun in 1890, also popularized the delicacy and tastefulness of the small oyster for natives and visiting legislators alike.

In 1893 the Brenner family built their first oyster processing plant on East Fourth Street, which was replaced in 1927 by a new building. In 1951, Brenner, as well as other oystermen, moved closer to the beds at Oyster Bay.

In 1900 oystermen began damming the natural tidelands to create more extensive beds for the culturing of oysters.

The cultivation of oysters was a resounding success, which brought production from a low of 24,000 bushels in 1910 to a high of 50,000 bushels in 1924. By 1921, oyster growers were experiencing a surplus, and started an advertising campaign. Unfortunately the decline of the oyster coincided with the influx of sulfite pulp mill waste from area mills and by 1955 only 3,500 bushels were being harvested.

Beginning in the 1920s Japanese Pacific oysters were introduced into lower Puget Sound waters with great success. Recently the Olympia oyster has made a significant comeback as environmental restrictions have improved its habitat. The harvest of oysters and clams now adds $4 million to the local economy. "Old Olympia" photos from the Jeffers Studio Collection

The busy Port of Olympia is shown here circa 1925 after the completion of tracks and wharves.

Spurred by the dredging and filling of the Olympia harbor, Thurston County established a port district in November 1922. The early years were spent building wharves and additional filling.

In 1925 the first vessels loaded lumber at the port and by 1927, ninety ships were calling at Olympia. In 1929 over 228 million board feet of lumber were shipped aboard 224 vessels calling at Olympia. Photo courtesy of the Port of Olympia

The Washington Veneer plant was the second large plywood mill on the port fill which boasted a brick smokestack 225 feet high. The stack was the pride of Olympia before the era of pollution control.

To dedicate the stack, the company sponsored a contest to guess the number of bricks and even staged a wedding on top of the stack in June 1925. The event spurred a host of activities including a parade down Main Street led by the Fort Lewis Band. Carrier pigeons and a newsreel camera stood by as the couple was lifted inside the smokestack along with a minister who performed the unique ceremony.

The smokestack was torn down in the 1960s. State Capital Museum photo

Inspired by the exploits of Charles Lindbergh, Olympians as many of their fellow countrymen, were determined to enter the air age. Recalling the siting of the railroads, city fathers decided Olympia was not to be left off the main line again. Members of the Chamber of Commerce purchased the Tumwater prairie where barnstormers had been landing, for an airport.

Another plan was also hatched to put Olympia on the aviation map. In 1927 the National Air Race was to be held between New York and Spokane. A Seattle flyer persuaded the Olympians to enter the "City of Olympia" in the race. The Woodson 16 with a Detroit Air Cat engine was to be flown by a navy-trained flyer who was to test the northern aviation route which could include

Olympia. Alas, the plane crashed outside Napoleon, Ohio, where it was built.

A bond issue was passed in November 1928 to buy the airport property and Olympia entered the air age. The city installed a beacon at the airport and planned one atop the capitol dome in Olympia, but nevertheless was excluded from the main route of the airways.

The airport has been operated by the Port of Olympia since 1963. Photo courtesy of Dewey Martin

Hugh Jeffers was welcomed by fellow flying enthusiasts on his arrival in Olympia from Colorado in the 1920s. "Old Olympia" photo from the Jeffers Studio

These women were busy touting t[he] many products native to Washingt[on] for the Women's Club in 1920. The[y] are shown here outside the clubhouse on Washington Street. Henderson House Museum photo

The Schmidt House, called "Three Meter" by the family, was built originally in 1895 when the brewe[ry] was constructed. The large wing was added in the 1920s. The Gree[k] influence is echoed in the statues [on] the lawn. The house overlooks Bu[dd] Inlet and a pathway leads to the brewhouse.

The house is part of the Tumwat[er] Historic District which is on the National Register of Historic Place[s.] Schmidt House Collection photo

Located near the present Tumwate[r] Freeway interchange, the Olympi[c] Auto Camp under the proprietorsh[ip] of the Trosper family offered cotta[ges,] kitchen, laundry and individual stoves for 250 visitors. Boasting twenty-one lakes and four rivers within half an hour's drive, the car[p] charged fifty cents per day for tent[s,] a dollar per day per car for cottage[s] and twenty-five cents per car for th[e] use of fuel and stoves. Henderson House Museum photo

Local Laceyites gathered in front of their railroad station in the 1920s. Lacey Plywood now occupies the site of the station. Lacey Museum photo

A parish was formed during the construction of the first St. Martin's buildings to serve construction workers and area residents near St. Martin's monastery.

The Sacred Heart Church was built in 1922 on Adams Road in Lacey. Lacey Museum photo

The second St. Peter's Hospital was built in 1924 on the west side of Olympia when the Capitol Grounds expanded. The hospital expanded again in the 1970s to a site near Lacey. Currently the hospital is used for low-cost apartments. Photo courtesy of St. Peter's Hospital

The Liberty Theater opened in August 1924 as a vaudeville house. Reed-Ingham Investment built the theater building which was on the Reed family home site. More than 2,000 theatergoers attended the premier, which featured a moving picture, vaudeville act, and organ concert on the mighty Wurlitzer. The theater was managed by longtime theater impresario W. G. McDonald. Later the theater hosted the Governor's Festival of the Arts in the 1960s. The site of the thea is now the Washington Center. "Old Olympia" photo from Jeffers Studio

Built for longtime theater owners, the Zabel family, the Capitol opened just after the Liberty in October 1924. The building with its distinctive cornice and leaded glass windows was designed by Joseph Wohleb. The theater has hosted a number of premieres including "Tugboat Annie" and "Ring of Fire." Built as a vaudeville house, the building has also hosted a number of local stage productions. "Old Olympia" photo from Jeffers Studio

The wooden buildings at St. Martin's were replaced with the present brick structures beginning in 1913. Construction was completed in the 1920s.

St. Martin's has long been the cultural and educational center of Lacey and is a hilltop landmark in the area. Lacey Museum photo

The St. Martin's lads were treated as Lacey's own as the townsfolk came out for their sporting events and activities. Here the locals and beanie-clad St. Martin's students cheer the competitors on to victory. Lacey Museum photo

Father Sebastian Ruth at St. Martin's was pioneering radio on the college campus while it was expanding.

Father Sebastian received his first license in 1914 and received his call letters of "7YS" in 1916. He broadcast as a telegraph station from St. Martin's with his transmitter of five watts until 1921. In the summer of 1921, he began experiments in voice transmission, joining a few other early radio pioneers. St. Martin's College photo

By January 1922 area listeners could look forward to regular programming on Sunday, Tuesday, and Friday evenings from a small wireless shack on the campus. In April 1922, Father Sebastian was issued "KGY" call numbers; his was only the 110th station in the United States.

Father Sebastian brought a wide variety of programming, ranging from opera to live performances, to his little station at St. Martin's. The station was sold to commercial interests in 1932 but Father Sebastian continued his amateur radio broadcasting until his death in 1958. He was honored as one of the pioneers in northwest radio. St. Martin's College photo

As in most communities, the automobile made a big impact on the way of life in the Capital Community by making people more mobile, changing the shape of downtowns, and sounding the death knell for the steamers on the sound and the streetcars and railroads on land.

Shown here is the Bronson Motor Car Co. which was located at 602 East Fourth Street in 1921. State Capital Museum photo

On May 1926, thirty-seventh anniversary of the establishment of the telephone exchange, the company's first patrons gathered for a photograph. Shown are Charles Springer, Mrs. Fannie O'Brien, C. R. Talcott, C. J. Lord, Frank Kenny, Mrs. Jevens, Mr. Filkey, Harry McElroy, G. N. Talcott, Burt Borgens, Grant Talcott, and Arly Van Epps.

The exchange was located at Fifth and Franklin. State Capital Museum photo

The celebration of May Day in Sylvester Park was a gala affair complete with trumpeters and a queen. Catherine Redpath was crowned in this 1924 photo taken at the gazebo. Photo from the Olympia High School Yearbook, courtesy of Catherine Weller

This picture was taken looking east on Fifth Avenue, circa 1925. "Old Olympia" photo from Jeffers Studio

This picture was taken looking west on Fifth with the new Capitol Theater in the foreground. "Old Olympia" photo from Jeffers Studio

Governor Roland Hartley places the capstone atop the legislative building on October 14, 1926. At last Olympia had its permanent capitol. Tacoma Public Library photo

Governor Hartley posed in front of the Governor's Mansion in his motor car circa 1928. State Capital Museum photo

The Capital

The coveted title of "Capital" has been jealously guarded and fought for all through Olympia's history.

The stage was set for the creation of Washington Territory in 1846 when the boundary was established by treaty with Great Britain between Canada and the United States. Oregon Territory was designated in 1848 but the northern section of the territory felt isolated from the government south of the Columbia River. After a series of meetings and petitions, President Franklin Pierce signed the legislation on March 2, 1853 creating Washington Territory (Residents had asked for the name to be "Columbia" but they were overruled in Washington, D.C.).

When first territorial governor Isaac I. Stevens arrived in Washington in November 1853, he called for the first legislature to meet in Olympia, which boasted the customs house and only territorial newspaper as well as a significant population. This first legislative body met in February 1854 in the Parker and Colter Building built by Edmund Sylvester with a recently added story to accommodate the meeting at its Second and Main location.

The Masonic temple at Seventh and Capitol street served as the meeting hall for the December 1854 session and in 1855, Olympia was named permanent capital. Construction under a $5000 grant from the federal government on a capitol building got under way later that year but was interrupted by the Indian Uprising. Not until the fourth assembly of 1856-57 did the solons meet in the territorial capitol.

Although the building was located at Olympia, the jealousies of other towns wanting the prestige and economic benefits of capital life soon intervened. Vancouver, supported by Portland, Oregon, wanted the capital and almost succeeded in 1859-60. In the 1860-61 legislative session the Vancouver forces did succeed in passing a capital relocation bill with a referendum to the people attached. However, someone (and there are stories it might have been Olympia partisans) neglected to incorporate the legally necessary enacting clause on the bill. Olympia and Vancouver were the sites of a split legislature and Supreme Court for a time, but the court decided in favor of Olympia, as did the people, when

The Gold Bar Restaurant, shown here in its declining years, circa 1903, was the site of the first Territorial Legislature in 1854. The building was constructed by Edmund Sylvester for the Parker & Colter Store and was the largest meeting place in the small frontier town in 1854.

The building was moved and later torn down in 1911. A plaque was installed at 222 N. Capitol Way in 1912 by the Washington State Historical Society, marking its former location.

Wood from the building was used to build two models of the structure which served as the first Capitol Building. One is on display at the State Capital Museum and the other at the Office of the Superintendent of Public Instruction. State Capital Museum photo

Governor Isaac Stevens' home on the north end of the present grounds was built in 1856 and was later used by first state Governor Elisha Ferry. The house was razed in 1929 over the objections of Kate Stevens Bates, daughter of Isaac Stevens. A marker stands at the site erected by the Daughters of the American Revolution, Sacajawea Chapter. State Capital Museum photo

Olympia handily won the statewide referendum.

With the advent of statehood in 1889, the capital controversy again heated up. Olympia had been left behind in population, railroads, and development; Ellensburg and North Yakima saw their chance to be capital. However a referendum for capital location included with the general constitution vote again favored Olympia.

The problem of a permanent building for the state capitol remained unsettled. In 1893 the State Capitol Commission decided to sell some of the 132,000 acres of timberland set aside under the statehood grant to build a capitol. However, economic conditions were poor after a depression that year, and no buyers were forthcoming. Architect Ernest Flagg's design was stopped at the foundation.

The wooden capitol was becoming more and more tumble-down and in 1901 Governor John Rogers purchased the Thurston County Courthouse for $350,000 which was to have a wing built for legislative chambers. That process was not completed in time for the 1903 session and the lawmakers met in the Farquhar Store building usually used as an armory, but to the embarrassment of Olympians was dubbed "The Barn" by visiting legislators.

By 1905 the resplendent sandstone capitol was ready. Tacoma lawmakers sponsored yet another referendum bill to move the capital but it was vetoed by then Governor Mead.

By 1911 those quarters were already cramped and a competition was held to establish a new design for the capitol building. A novel group concept was advocated and Wilder and White, noted New York architects won the competition. All of the buildings on the West Campus have similar architectural features and are constructed of Wilkeson sandstone quarried forty miles east of Olympia. The buildings are meant to form a base for the mammoth sized dome so at a distance they appear to be one structure. The general plan was to be symmetrical, although some of the buildings of the original design were never built while others have been added. The landscaping of the West Campus was designed by the famous Olmsted Brothers of Brookline, Massachusetts who developed the plan in 1927.

The campus expanded across Capitol Way during the 1960s when a new series of buildings was built around an open terraced plaza which softened the stark concrete with large planting beds, modern sculpture and trees. A state law passed in 1974 allowed for one-half of one percent of the total cost of new buildings to be used for public art which enabled the placement of the fine pieces seen on the East Campus.

The Masonic temple at the corner of Eighth and Capitol was the site of the Territorial Legislature during the Indian Uprising in 1855-1856.

The impressive structure served many civic uses including schools and public meetings.

The Masonic temple was the first organized in the Territory and first met on the south side of Olympia Street, between Capitol Way and Washington Street, marked as Olympia Lodge No. 1 of the F and AM of Washington. State Capital Museum photo

After the disruption of the Indian Uprising the wooden capitol was completed in 1856. Congress had appropriated $5,000 for a capitol building with the creation of the Territory. Although Stevens convened the first legislature in the Olympia in 1854, it was not until 1855 that the permanent capital was established in Olympia.

The building, measuring forty feet by sixty-eight feet, housed the legislative chambers, committee rooms, and the territorial library.

Located near the present legislative building, the site is marked by a plaque on its northeast corner, set under the aegis of the Daughters of the American Revolution. State Capital Museum photo

On Statehood Day, November 18, 1889, the wooden capitol was arrayed in bunting and evergreens but the need became apparent for a more fitting structure to house state government than the cramped wooden building.

In approving the state constitution in 1889, President Harrison also stipulated that 132,000 acres of federal lands within the state be set aside, the proceeds from which were to be used for the "erection of buildings at the state capital."

Olympians, always anxious to please the state, had donated $2,500 for an addition to the old wooden structure to house the Constitutional Convention in 1889. State Capital Museum photo

Governor John Rogers breaks ground for the east wing of the newly purchased state capitol, circa 1901.

Because of the difficulty in financing a new building through the sale of timber, Governor Rogers decided to purchase the grand towered Thurston County Courthouse for $350,000. The east wing was to house the legislative chambers. State Capital Museum photo

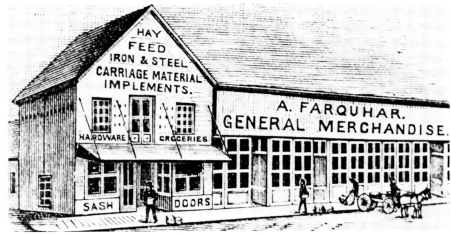

Unfortunately the additions to the courthouse were not complete in time for the 1903 legislative session and instead of meeting in the dilapidated wooden capitol on the hill, the legislators met in yet another temporary capitol, the Farquhar Store. It was constructed in 1890 for A. Farquhar at Seventh and Adams on land which he had purchased from Michael Simmons. The building had been used as a general store, an armory, and feed and seed store. Unappreciative legislators called it "The Barn." State Capital Museum photo

This is the old Capitol after the completion of the east wing, which was ready for occupancy by the 1905 legislative session. Both the original Chuckanut sandstone and the new Tenino sandstone east wing were designed by architect Willis Ritchie in the Richardson Romanesque style architecture. He incorporated many technical innovations including steel framing and elevators. The chambers for the first time had room for spectators to witness the legislative action.

On the first floor of the original buildings were the offices of governor, auditor, treasurer, and attorney general. The annex housed the land commissioner, school superintendent, secretary of state, and bureau of labor. The second floor originally hosted the supreme court and state library.

A 1930s public works project cut the height of the second floor chambers and other floors were partitioned as well.

The building suffered damage by fire in 1928 and also in the 1949 earthquake. During 1981-83 a major renovation project was undertaken to clean and restore the structure. Two new elevators were installed,

The old Capitol Building continued to house the majority of state agencies until 1919 when other buildings were erected on the present campus. The legislature met in the structure until September 1928, when fire gutted the tower and caused other damage.

The earthquake of 1949 resulted in the loss of ten of the twelve towers. It eliminated the rotunda and damaged the chambers and galleries in the east wing. State Capital Museum photo

skylights were uncovered, and a new copper roof was put into place. The main stairs and corridors were once again opened as in the original. The Superintendent of Public Instruction of Washington now occupies the building which opened again in February 1983 after the $9 million renovation. State Capital Museum photo

This was the interior of the old Capitol with busy employees, circa 1915. State Capital Museum photo

Topping the crest to the west of the Legislative Building is the Governor's Mansion. Built in 1908, it is the oldest of the campus buildings. The Georgian red brick residence was designed by Tacoma architects Russell & Babcock and boasts one of the best collections of American antique furniture in the United States, including some original Duncan Phyfe pieces.

Renovated and enlarged in 1974, the building serves as residence for the Washington governor. Del Ogden photo

The Temple of Justice across the oval from the Legislative Building was the first of the Capitol Group to be completed, and set the tone for the design and style of all of the other pieces. Begun in 1912, the building was completed in stages because of difficulties in financing. Like most of the other buildings, its structural walls are of brick and although the building was the site of the inaugural ball of Governor Lister in 1913, its raw brick walls remained exposed until 1917 when they were faced with sandstone. Not until 1920 was the interior finishing completed.

The building houses the nine justices of the Supreme Court, their staff, the main office of the attorney general, and an extensive legal library. State Capital Museum photo

The Insurance Building was the second of the Wilder and White designs built on campus. Completed in 1920 for general offices, the sandstone building retains a common height and roofline so as not to detract from the Legislative Building. Colonnading similar to that structure is evident on the south and north ends where bronze railings have a ship, tree, and state seal insignias. The Insurance Commissioner, Office of Financial Management, and Fire Marshall are located here. A parallel structure to the Insurance Building but west of the Legislative Building was part of the Wilder and White plan but was never built. State Capital Museum photo

One of the early photos of the construction of the Legislative Building which was begun as the crowning element of the Capitol Group in 1923. The foundations encompassed the Flagg structures built in 1893. The foundation is Index granite from Index, Washington. That material was also used for the terrace floor, steps, platforms, sills, and doorways.

Shown here also is the 130-foot square pad of concrete and reinforced steel, over 22 feet deep, which supports the dome.

Done in 1922, this pad required a monumental effort in the high technology of the day. The monolithic concrete pouring to assure strength lasted four straight days and nights. Through this pad the piers transfer the thirty-ton weight of the dome to the subsoil below. State Capital Museum photo

This stone carver was at work on the Corinthian capitals at the main entrance. At one time over 500 workers were on the site and the building project set in motion a worldwide search for marble setters and stone carvers. John Bruce, chief of carvers, who received $125 per week, had about thirty assistants. Carving was done with hand tools and sandblasting equipment. The master carver worked the first design from plaster models and the assistants duplicated his work. State Capital Museum photo

The columns were marching along the facade in this 1924 view of the construction. Most of the columns are four feet in diameter and twenty-five feet high, created in a simplified Doric style around the colonnade. The columns on the main north entrance (shown here) and the south portico are slightly taller, measuring thirty feet in height and four feet in diameter with ornate Corinthian capitals. State Capital Museum photo

The most outstanding element of the building is the dome soaring 287 feet above the terrace of the main structure, taller than the dome of any other state capitol.

The dome is supported by four piers nineteen feet square with four-foot thick walls rising eighty feet high, resting on a concrete pad.

Another pad on top of the piers supports the thirty-three-foot high drum of the dome. Above the drum the Corinthian columns measuring thirty-one feet set the stage for the dome itself. The capitals on the dome colonnade were carved on the ground before placement and their design resembles the Pantheon in Rome.

The dome is actually three domes: one of lath and plaster (seen from the rotunda), the exterior one of brick and stone, and an unseen steel and concrete cone between the two. A one-half inch gap between the outer dome and the lantern's concrete slab is lined with greased lead which allows the outer dome to expand or contract without affecting the lantern.

The 1,400 cut stones of the dome presented a challenge to stone-cutters since none of the stones has a straight line on any edge or face. A specially designed cutter which cut stone from two sides was used, and when the last stone was placed on October 13, 1926, three-eighths of an inch projected on all sides, which was the exact specification in the architectural drawings! State Capital Museum photo

The Senate chamber to the east of the rotunda reflects the grandeur of the interior of the building with its dramatic Fomosa marble in reddish-grey tones from Germany. The book-faced marble cutting technique creates on the pillars the look of evergreen trees symbolizing Washington, the Evergreen State. The Senate furnishings, including the desks and hand-carved rostrum, are mahogany and were designed by architects Wilder and White. Del Ogden photo

A view of the Legislative Building shortly after its completion in 1928 shows the landscaping done by the famed Olmsted Brothers of Brookline, Massachusetts.

Constructed of brick faced with stone on the exterior and marble on the interior, the Legislative Building measures 413 feet long and 179.2 feet wide and is the equivalent of thirty stories in height.

The sandstone for the structure was quarried at Wilkeson, forty miles east of Olympia. State Capital Museum photo

The Transportation Building is one of the two structures south of the Legislative Building which were part of the original Wilder and White plan. They are arranged to form a courtyard with the Legislative Building. Called a "spearhead design," they have a diagonal orientation with the fronts of the spearheads at the far east and west of the buildings which have colonnades matching the Legislative Building. An underground tunnel joins the two buildings.

Built in 1940 under the FERA program of the Roosevelt Administration, the building is constructed of reinforced concrete with the familiar Wilkeson sandstone. State Capital Museum photo

This is an aerial view of the Legislative Building and Temple of Justice. Del Ogden photo

The first of the memorials to dead soldiers on the campus, this World War I memorial was designed in brass by Victor Alonzo Lewis in 1938. Three larger-than-life fighting men and a Red Cross nurse are under the protective care of a winged victory figure standing twelve feet high. State Capital Museum photo

Beginning in the 1960s the expansion of state government mandated the expansion of the campus to the east of Capitol Way.

The open terraced plaza shown here covers an extensive parking garage. Surrounding the green space are high-rise offices built between 1961 and 1976. The prize-winning landscape design softens the stark concrete with large planting beds, modern sculpture, and a variety of trees.

At left is the Transportation Building of 1970 and at right the Employment Security Building of 1961. Del Ogden photo

The Legislative Building is lit nightly, creating an impressive sight as seen here from the eastern approach under the plaza. At left is Office Building II. Del Ogden photo

A state law passed in 1974 allowed for one half of one percent of the total cost of new buildings to be used for public art.

Lee Kelly's giant burnished stainless steel slabwork fronts the Transportation Building as part of that program. Del Ogden photo

The Capital Brewery buildings were the first structures built by Leopold Schmidt for his new brewery in 1896. The name of the brewery was changed to "Olympia Brewery" in 1902.

Buildings of the original brewery included a small one-story ice factory powered by the lower falls, a four-story wooden brewhouse, a five-story cellar building, and also a bottling and keg plant. State Capital Museum photo

The Olympia Brewing Company and The Olympia-Tumwater Foundation

The falls of the Deschutes River at Tumwater, formed by a volcanic flow which turned to basalt perhaps fifty million years ago, have been a center for human activities for hundreds of years. Native peoples camped around the falls using the site as a food processing area. The first European inhabitants of the area, the Hudson's Bay Company, established the falls as a rendezvous point on voyages connecting their northwest settlements.

It was at the mouth of the Deschutes River that the first permanent American settlers on Puget Sound—the Simmons-Bush Party—located in the fall of 1845. The Americans quickly set about using the falls to power first a gristmill and then a sawmill. Other manufacturers quickly followed so that by the 1880s the falls were lined with water driven industries. However, by the 1890s many of the buildings had burned, some of the early businesses had relocated, and difficult economic times had taken their toll. It was to this site that Leopold Schmidt came in 1895 also attracted by the falls of the Deschutes River.

German-born, Leopold F. Schmidt was trained in Europe as a seaman in his early years but ventured to the United States in the 1860s. He went first to the Great Lakes and then to Montana where he established the Centennial Brewery in Butte. Schmidt honed his brewing skills at the Worms Brewing Academy in Germany and returned to Montana. Later as a member of the Montana Capitol Commission, Schmidt visited Olympia and heard of the artesian water at Tumwater and the nearby falls. He sent samples of the water to Chicago's Wahl-Henius Brewer's Institute. The results of the tests indicated that the water was exceptional for brewing with perfect solvent characteristics, similar to the noted water in Burton-Upon-Trent in England.

Schmidt, who had a love for the sea, liked the location of the falls of the Deschutes, near salt water. Readily available power and shipping facilities were also nearby. In late 1895, after liquidating his interest in the Butte brewery, Schmidt purchased five acres at the former site of the Biles and Carter Tannery where an ice plant was already located. On the site were good houses, an orchard, and thirty horsepower of waterpower. He paid James Bile's widow Fannie $4,500 for the site and waterpower rights from the falls.

On October 1, 1896, the Capital Brewery produced the first "Olympia Pale Export" beer from the new facility. Schmidt at first was unsure of how well the enterprise would fare. However, the brewery was tremendously successful, growing from a production of 4,255 barrels in 1897 to 49,800 in 1904 and sales rising from $28,276 to $500,000 during that time. To keep up with demand, Schmidt built a large brick brewhouse in 1906, which still stands ninety years later.

The business grew continuously until Mr. Schmidt, and Olympia Brewing Company as it came to be known after 1902, controlled five breweries in Washington, Oregon, and California—the Bellingham Bay Brewery, built in 1902, the Salem Brewery in Oregon, added in 1904, the Acme Brewery in San Francisco, built in 1906 after the earthquake and fire, and the Port Townsend Brewery, established in 1909. However, Schmidt noted that none of the other breweries could produce the same beer as the Tumwater facility because of the unique qualities of the water at that location. He used the water not only in brewing but also throughout the operation. Olympia Beer was produced only at the Tumwater location. The Olympia Brewery was also notable for the cleanliness and sanitation of every part of the plant, this due to Mr. Schmidt's scientific training in brewing.

With the vote for Prohibition in Washington in 1914, all production of beer was required to cease by December 31, 1915. Leopold Schmidt who died in 1914 did not live to see Prohibition. However, his family carried on in business. Beginning in 1916, the Schmidt family turned to producing fruit juices, jam, and jellies at the brewery. By 1921 this was also halted. The brewery buildings were sold to a company which developed a pulp and paper rolling mill on the site. This enterprise was shortlived and closed shortly after opening in 1929. The Schmidts then invested in other interests in the hotel, creamery, and transportation arenas. However, the family was careful to preserve the Olympia Brewing Company name, trademark, and "It's the Water" slogan in anticipation of the lifting of Prohibition.

With the end of Prohibition in 1933, Leopold Schmidt's sons, Peter and Adolph Sr., both experienced brewmasters, decided to re-establish the brewery at a location near the old plant. While the pre-Prohibition facility was inadequate for a modern brewery, they wanted to be close to the artesian water sources. On January 14, 1934, the re-formed Olympia Brewing Company celebrated the first beer out of the bottlehouse. The newly-constituted brewery grew rapidly, especially after World War II when restrictions on materials were lifted. By 1956 Olympia Brewing Company passed the 1,000,000 barrel production mark with Peter G. Schmidt at its helm.

In the 1950s Peter Schmidt, the Schmidt family, and close associates established The Olympia-Tumwater Foundation, formed to provide a variety of charitable projects for the community and scholarships to area students. The first venture of the Foundation was the donation of the Tivoli Fountain to the people of Washington. The dream of Peter Schmidt, the fountain was built on the Washington State Capitol Campus in 1953. It is a duplicate of a fountain at Tivoli Gardens in Copenhagen, Denmark. The Olympia-Tumwater Foundation also de-

Leopold Frederick Schmidt was born in Dornassen-heim, Oberhesse, Germany in 1846. At age fourteen Leopold started his seamanship training with the Hamburg American Line. After sailing to European ports with ships of the firm, he came to the United States in 1866. Schmidt first went to the German community in Augusta, Missouri, and then sailed on ships in the Great Lakes. Caught up in the excitement of the gold rush, he journeyed to Montana in 1870.

After a trip up the Missouri River to Ft. Benton, Leopold walked overland to Helena, Montana, and then to Butte where the mining boom was on in earnest. Leopold, however, constructed sluice boxes for the miners. A Frenchman, Pierre Valiton, who was brewing beer in a makeshift facility and selling it to the miners, recruited Schmidt to operate his business while he was on an extended absence. On Valiton's return to Butte, Schmidt decided to gain more knowledge about brewing. He returned to Germany and enrolled in Worms Brewing Academy and apprenticed in German breweries. He returned to Butte with his German wife, Johanna Steiner Schmidt, in 1879. There he established the Centennial Brewing Company which over time prospered with branches in Glendale and Anaconda, Montana.

Active politically, Schmidt became a member of the constitutional convention for Montana, a county commissioner, and a representative in the legislature. It was in his role as capitol commissioner for Montana that he visited Olympia in 1894 and envisioned the possibilities for a brewery at the falls of the Deschutes.

Seeing business opportunities in the Pacific Northwest, Schmidt decided to liquidate his interest in the Centennial Brewery in Butte. He located his family in Portland, Oregon, while he established the Capital Brewery at Tumwater. Schmidt moved his family to Olympia in 1897. All of Leopold and Johanna Schmidt's five sons eventually worked at the brewery.

Leopold Schmidt maintained his Montana connections and remained an astute entrepreneur looking for opportunities throughout his life. He was, however, known as a scrupulously honest businessman and promoted the temperate consumption of his product. His motto served the brewery well, "Quality First—Quantity Second." At the time of his death, Schmidt was president of the Olympia National Bank and held interests in the Olympus Hotel in Tacoma and his namesake Leopold Hotel in Bellingham. Schmidt was noted as a being "invariably generous" and donated the Swiss chalet which stood for many years at Priest Point Park in Olympia. It was originally erected at the Lewis and Clark Exposition in Portland as the Brewery Pavilion. Schmidt who died in 1914 and his wife Johanna who died three years earlier are interred near the Schmidt home in Tumwater.

veloped Tumwater Falls Park in 1962-1963 along the historic Deschutes River Falls.

In order to accommodate continued demand, the Brewery expanded and mechanized its bottle and keg facilities east of the Deschutes River in the 1960s. The firm reached the two-million-barrel mark of annual production in 1964.

The Brewery also developed a 260-acre recreational facility along the Deschutes River of an eighteen-hole golf course, clubhouse, and athletic complex which was completed in 1970.

The Olympia Brewing Company purchased Hamm's Brewery of St. Paul, Minnesota, in 1975 and Lone Star Brewing Company of San Antonio, Texas, in 1976 in order to stay competitive nationally. However, national economic forces within the brewing industry adversely affected Olympia Brewing Company. In 1983 Pabst Brewing Company purchased all of the shares of the company, including the shares owned by the Schmidt family, which ended the long association of the family with Olympia Brewing Company. At the time that Olympia Brewing Company was sold to Pabst, production at the Tumwater

plant had reached a peak of three million barrels per year with total national production, including the Tumwater, St. Paul, and San Antonio Plants, of 5.5 million annual barrels, at which time Olympia Brewing Company was number six in production among American brewers.

The Olympia-Tumwater Foundation obtained the Schmidt family home, Three Meter, and the historic archives of the brewery. The family interests continue in The Olympia-Tumwater Foundation which remains active especially in the administration of Tumwater Falls Park, scholarship, and research programs. Under the ownership of Pabst Brewing Company, the Olympia facility in 1995 produced 2.7 million barrels of beer which was marketed as approximately twelve brands. The facility continues to be one of area's largest employers.

Pictured are the Schmidt Family circa 1897. In the top row, left to right, are: Frank, Peter G., Leopold F. Jr., and Adolph Sr. In the bottom row, left to right, are: Frederick, Leopold F., Philippine, and Johanna Schmidt.

First production from the Capital Brewery was on October 1, 1896. The decorated streetcar came from the brewery at Tumwater. Pictured from left to right are Charles Helm, a Tacoma restaurateur, Henry Schupp, a close friend and business partner of Schmidt's, Leopold Schmidt, and A. W. Wolf, secretary of the company. The streetcar is just in front of the McKenny Block.

First letterhead of Capital Brewing Company showing the signature of Leopold Schmidt.

The early labels of the brewery already featured the falls of the Deschutes and the lucky horseshoe. They were produced by the Louis Roesch Company of San Francisco.

Early advertising was a genteel variety. The Schmidt family stressed that their product was a light and moderate libation. The Schmidt's were not blind to promotion however. The Capital Brewing Company sent six barrels packed with Olympia Beer to Admiral George Dewey and the crew of the flagship Olympia after their victory in the decisive battle of Manila Bay on July 3, 1898.

The Olympia Brewery grew rapidly, outpacing the eastern beers in sales. The new plant at the falls was enlarged many times. In the 1890s, Schmidt put a high premium on his product selling the beer for $8.00 per barrel when the going rate was $3.25. The house to the right of the photograph was known as "Hillside Inn" by members of the Schmidt Family.

The Italianate brewhouse which was built in 1906 was designed and engineered by the Vilter Company of Milwaukee, Wisconsin. The ornate brickwork was created by the artisans who built the structure.

The brewery held a contract with Olympia Light and Power Company to haul draught beer to the bottling plant and bottled beer to Percival's Dock for shipment. Pictured are motorman "Shorty," "Duke," who ran the hospitality room, and in the background Fred Brey, brewery yardman, circa 1905. The brewery generated electricity to run the refrigeration equipment and all of the pumps by burning Tenino coal in a gas producer developed by Leopold's oldest son, Peter. The gas produced provided the fuel for engines which ran electric generators. Excess power that was generated was fed into the streetcar line to provide part of the electrical power to run the streetcars.

The Olympia Brewhouse after completion was a six-story Italianate style structure set on a concrete base. Built of Chehalis brick, the building had a copper roof, a large central door fashioned in Tenino sandstone, and a unique commercial style. Adjoining the main brewery were storage sheds and a cooperage. The Northern Pacific Railroad extended a line to the Brewhouse in 1906 as seen at the left of the photograph.

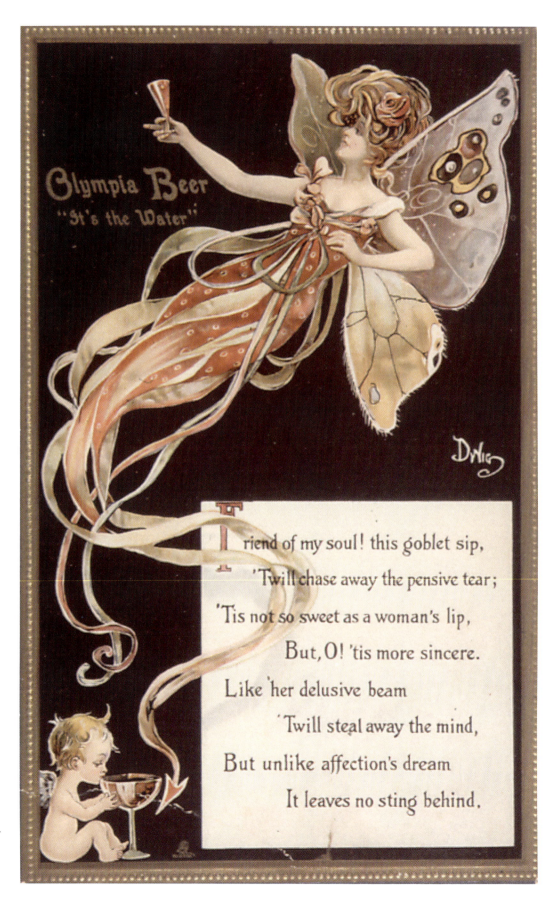

Another example of the fanciful and wholesome advertising of the company from the turn of the century.

By 1902 the name of the Brewery had been changed to Olympia Brewing Company from Capital Brewing Company. It was also in 1902 that the slogan, "It's the Water" was adopted, shown here on a label.

It was the idea of Frank M. Kenney who was the secretary, office and advertising manager of the company. He thought the uniqueness of the water which made Olympia Beer so distinctive should be told in the slogan. He had to convince Leopold Schmidt but it served the company well.

Hygeian Spring Water Label

Hand-tinted color postcard of the brewery showing the wharves and brick brewhouse with Three-Meter on the bank above, 1912.

The Schmidt family home, Three Meter, was built in 1904 by carpenter Albert MacIntosh who also worked at the brewery. How the elegant old home earned the nickname "Three Meter" is the subject of lengthy Schmidt family debates. Pictured here in front of the house is a group of vendors for Olympia Beer on an excursion to the Brewery in 1907. Seated in the center is Leopold Schmidt.

This shows the new brewhouse looking west toward Tumwater across the railroad bridge. State Capital Museum photo

Appleju Label

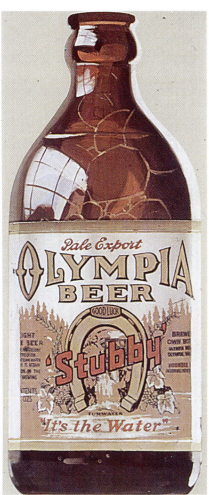

The Olympia Beer "Stubby" bottle was developed and introduced in 1936. Its short neck and wide body protected the flavor of the beer while its stronger walls facilitated pasteurization and shipping.

Olympia Brewery employees gathered here in 1903 to lift a stein of their handicraft. The Schmidt family established a kinship with their employees, who were unfailingly loyal to the family and company.

An Olympia Brewery delivery wagon at the loading dock was photographed in front of the brick brewhouse. Before the construction of Capitol Lake, the Deschutes basin was navigable up to these docks for the shipment of beer.

Shown is the Olympia Brewery Hospitality Room. One of the non-beer products of the Olympia Brewery was Olympia Hygeian Spring Water, which was bottled artesian water.

Another view shows the Deschutes Waterway and loading dock in front of the brewery.

Olympia Brewing Company advertising in the 1950s continued to stress the family nature of the beverage.

Construction on Tumwater Falls Park was begun in 1962 and completed in 1963 by The Olympia-Tumwater Foundation and Olympia Brewing Company. The fifteen-acre park encompasses the historic sites of the first permanent American settlement on Puget Sound and the first manufacturing sites utilizing the power of the falls. The park features a loop walkway along the three cataracts of the river. The design of the park was a collaboration between P. H. Schmidt, grandson of Leopold Schmidt, and Ray Prentice, a noted rockwork and landscape designer. Mr. Schmidt conceived and designed the office building and upper park area which features play structures and a picnic area. The arched bridge across the river was also designed by Mr. Schmidt. It is the east walkway where Mr. Prentice's artistry is evident. The rockwork falls which in some cases use recycled water from the brewery process were designed by Prentice who also landscaped the canyon. The walkways follow the falls giving glimpses of the extensive fishways which were built by the Washington Department of Fisheries in 1952. The fish handling facility for the harvesting of eggs is located adjacent to the upper falls. The Olympia-Tumwater Foundation owns and maintains the park which hosts 350,000 visitors annually. Photograph from the author's collection

Olympia Brewing Company was sold to Pabst Brewing Company in 1983. This aerial view of the modern brewery and picturesque Tumwater Falls Park is taken looking south to north over the complex with Olympia in the background. Photograph by Michael W. Siegrist Sr.

The marker dedicated by the descendants of Leopold Schmidt to the members of the first Permanent American Settlement on Puget Sound was first located in 1916 on Simmons Road near what is now Tumwater Historical Park. It was later relocated to upper falls area of Tumwater Falls Park.

The lucky horseshoe, the crest of the Schmidt family, has long been a symbol of the Olympia Brewery, here shown in festive style circa 1910, decked out for a Fourth of July in front of the Old Capitol in Olympia.

In 1914 Washington, Oregon, and Idaho voted for Prohibition. Breweries were required to cease operation by December 31, 1915. In 1916 Olympia Brewing Company turned to production of "Appleju," a juice drink made from Washington apples. They also produced jams, jellies, and preserves which were shipped to a nationwide market and overseas during World War I. The Salem Brewery produced "Loju," a loganberry drink product. By 1921 economic conditions forced the closure of the entire operation and the Schmidt family concentrated on other business interests. Shown is production of Appleju in Tumwater.

A landslide in 1902 demolished the bottleshop at the Tumwater Falls location. The bottleshop was moved for six years to a site near the Old Northern Pacific Depot on what is now the east side of Capitol Lake. During the years the bottling plant was located there, the beer was transported by streetcar to the bottling plant in sixty-three-gallon hogsheads on Olympia Light and Power Company streetcars. Olympia Brewery was the first on the coast to use the metal cap method of bottle sealing which made pasteurization of bottled beer possible. Pasteurization stops the yeast action and ensures sanitation.

Pictured is the brewery bottleshop, circa 1914. Bottles have the neck label "Vote Against Prohibition Bill No. 3." Herb Kane and Howard Stack are facing the camera while an unidentified inspector is seated. In about 1908, bottleshop crews put out from 40,000 to 60,000 bottles of beer each day. Brewery workers, who belonged to a union, received $4.00 a day wages which outpaced the going wage by $1.50.

Peter Schmidt, the eldest son of brewery founder Leopold Schmidt and his wife Johanna, very early became his father's right-hand. Born in 1880 in Montana, Schmidt came with his father in 1895 to Tumwater to build the original brewery and at age nineteen was made chief engineer of the company. He attended brewer's school in 1899 in Milwaukee and upon his return became brewmaster. By 1909 he was master brewer, general superintendent, and vice president of five Pacific Coast breweries.

Schmidt also founded Puget Sound Hotels, the precursor of Westin Hotels. Schmidt and his brother Adolph D. Schmidt Sr. formed Northwest Transportation Company which pioneered interstate bus service between Seattle and Portland. Peter Schmidt and another brother, Leopold Jr., also founded Pacific Highway Transport, one of the early heavy trucking firms to operate between the cities on the Pacific Highway in Washington and Oregon.

With the repeal of Prohibition in 1933, Schmidt with his brother Adolph Sr. re-established the Olympia Brewing Company. Selling stock at a dollar per share, the Schmidts put together one of the most modern breweries on the West Coast. Regarded as one of the nation's leading authorities of brewing technology, Peter Schmidt served as president of the brewery until 1953. The new Tumwater plant of Olympia Brewing Company was considered by many in the brewing industry to be one of the most modern, efficient, and clean breweries in the United States.

Locally Schmidt served eighteen years on the Olympia Port Commission and was instrumental in establishing the Olympia Airport. He was remembered as always excelling in the personal touch. He credited the success of Olympia Beer to "My father, my brothers and our associates"—meaning the employees of the Brewery. He and his wife Clara Muench Schmidt had five children. He died in 1957 and his wife died in 1960.

On October 1, 1936, the employees of the Olympia Brewing Company presented a plaque in memory of Leopold Schmidt and the founding of the Brewery forty years before. Left to right are: Frederick W. Schmidt, Peter G. Schmidt, Marion Camby who had worked at the old brewery, Norma Jean Simila, Lois Plamondon, (daughters of employees) Adolph Schmidt Sr., and Frank T. Schmidt.

Because of restrictions placed on raw materials during World War II, the metal caps used by the Brewery were recycled. Women replaced the men serving in the war by washing, sorting, and reshaping used bottle crowns. The crowns were then shipped to San Francisco where new cork was applied for use in bottling at the Olympia Plant. 1943 photograph.

At the close of Prohibition in 1933, Peter and Adolph Schmidt Sr. determined to re-open a new brewery utilizing the famous artesian water. Despite tough times, the brothers were able to raise enough money to begin the construction of a new modern brewery up the hill from the falls of the Deschutes River. Within 150 days the new plant was in full operation and the first post-Prohibition Olympia Beer was marketed on January 14, 1934. Many of the employees were those from pre-Prohibition days. Aerial photograph of the new plant, circa 1937.

181

Western Metal Craft took over the old brewhouse before World War II to build metal cabinets but by the 1950s had phased out their operations. Olympia Brewing Company purchased the old brewery buildings in 1964. Henderson House Museum photo

Washington Governor Arthur Langlie (right) and Peter G. Schmidt stand before the Tivoli Fountain on the Washington State Capitol Campus. The fountain is a replica of the one found in the Tivoli Park in Copenhagen, Denmark. The project which was the dream of Peter G. Schmidt was a gift to the state from The Olympia-Tumwater Foundation in 1953.

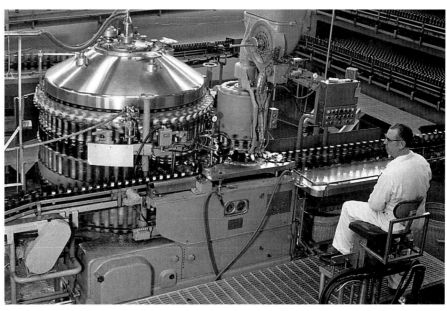

Born in 1912 to Adolph D. Sr. and Winifred Lang Schmidt, Adolph "Bump" Schmidt Jr. attended brewer's school and served as the brewmaster, superintendent, and vice president before succeeding his uncle, Peter G. Schmidt, as president of Olympia Brewing Company in 1953. A national leader in the brewery industry, he was also president of The Olympia-Tumwater Foundation. He was president of the company until 1963 and died in 1964. Schmidt was the grandson of Olympia Brewing Company founder Leopold Schmidt. Adolf "Bump" Schmidt's son, Leopold F. "Rick" Schmidt was later president of the Brewery from 1974 to 1979.

The modern mechanized bottling plant at the brewery contrasts with the modest operation at the turn of the century.

Robert A. "Bobby" Schmidt was born in 1915 to Adolph D. Sr. and Winifred Lang Schmidt. He started with Olympia Brewing Company when it was reorganized after the repeal of Prohibition. He served a full brewing apprenticeship and graduated from the United States Brewing Academy in New York. Robert A. Schmidt served as president of Olympia Brewing Company from 1963 until 1974. He resumed his position in 1979 as president, chief executive officer, and chairman of the Board in 1979 and again assumed the helm after James Senna in 1981-1982. He was president of the company when it was purchased by Pabst Brewing Company in 1983.

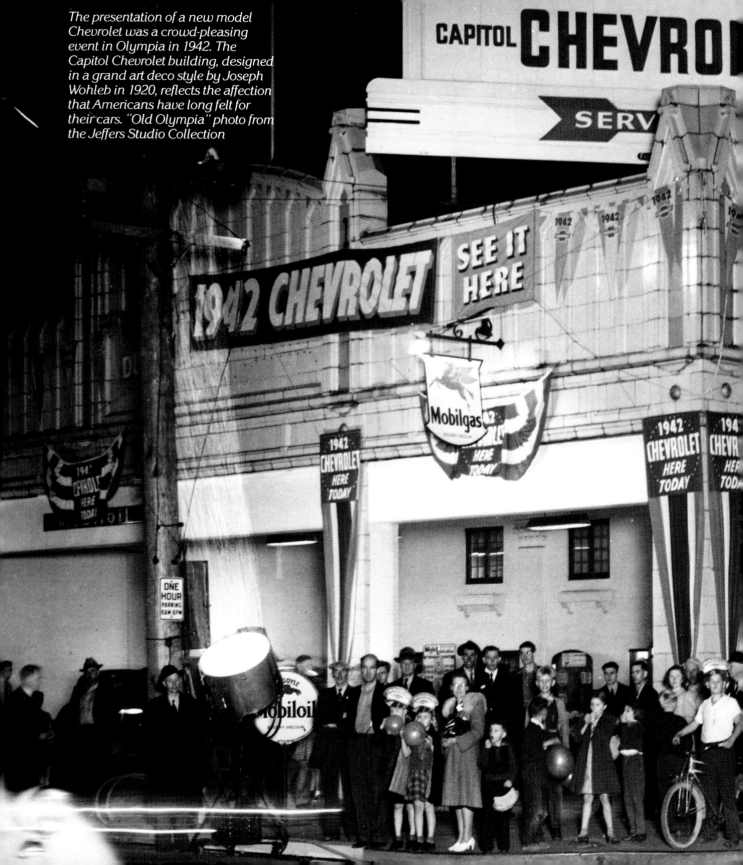

The presentation of a new model Chevrolet was a crowd-pleasing event in Olympia in 1942. The Capitol Chevrolet building, designed in a grand art deco style by Joseph Wohleb in 1920, reflects the affection that Americans have long felt for their cars. "Old Olympia" photo from the Jeffers Studio Collection

1930-1950

The Capital Community was affected much as the rest of the country with the onset of the Great Depression. The decade did begin with progress in building when the Governor House Hotel went up on the site of the former splendid Olympia. Thurston County built a new courthouse across from the Capitol Grounds that served the area until 1977. The structure, art deco in style, was constructed in solid Tenino sandstone in a design by noted local architect Joseph Wohleb. The *Daily Olympian* also erected a new building at the site of the former Burmeister Building at State Street and Capitol Way.

Poor economic straits affected many Olympians. The most visible was the advent of "Little Hollywood" on the east shores of what is now Capital Lake. The makeshift housing was symptomatic of the hard times Olympians were facing.

In 1933 a more strident group, the Republic of the Unemployed, marched on the Capitol in January of that year. A large group gathered in the old capitol building and sent a delegation to visit newly elected Governor Clarence D. Martin requesting unemployment insurance, disability allowances, hospital services, and a prohibition on foreclosures. Although the legislature enacted some relief measures yet another march took place in March 1933. This time the group was met by vigilantes who routed the group to Priest Point Park where they spent a damp and uncomfortable night surrounded by vigilantes and law enforcement officers. A delegation did see the governor, however.

A high point of 1933 in Olympia was the visit of the historic frigate, the *U.S.F. Constitution*. In its usual enthusiastic manner, the Olympia Chamber of Commerce decided to do up the visit of "Old Ironsides" right. Rebuilt a number of times, the ship had last been refurbished in 1925, eight years before. The Chamber issued $2000 worth of "Oyster Money" to commemorate the visit to be used at local businesses and to defray the costs of entertaining the officers and crew of the *Constitution*. Band concerts, a grand naval ball, luncheons, and private parties feted the guests during the ten-day visit. The ship logged its four millionth visitor as 39,000 people attended the festivities in Olympia.

Olympians bade farewell to the electric streetcars in the 1930s as they welcomed the new era of federal aid. The Social Security building on the Capitol Campus was

A new Thurston County Courthouse was built in 1930 on Capitol Way across from the main campus. The building was designed by Joseph Wohleb in an art deco style with a contingent of four eagles over the main entry. The substantial Tenino sandstone structure has withstood more than just the earthquakes and ravages of time. Slated for demolition in 1979, a grassroots effort helped place the structure on the National Register of Historic Places and thwarted plans for razing it. Plans for the building are uncertain but community leaders look forward to converting it into a Centennial Museum for Washington's State Centennial in 1989. State Capital Museum photo

built through Works Progress Administration (WPA) funds, and the WPA and War Emergency Relief Association conducted a number of projects at the Port of Olympia and the Olympia Airport.

Anticipating the war, the airport in Olympia became the site of the Civilian Pilot Training Program in 1939. The ground school was located at St. Martin's College as part of a national program to train pilots, radio operators, and mechanics. Some 1,150 people, men and women from all over the area, received training for the coming war.

The attack on Pearl Harbor was announced by the roof siren of the newly constructed Rockway-Leland Building which housed KGY radio. And with the strategic location of Olympia on the West Coast, an immediate volunteer corps of 200 women spotters was organized and the ladies also served in the Red Cross Motor Corps. An Army-Navy Club was organized on the first floor of the old capitol to accommodate the soldiers from nearby Ft. Lewis. Later a USO club was built on East Fourth Street which is now the Community Center. Citizens gathered scrap metal for the war effort and "grease matinees" were held at downtown theaters to aid the war effort.

During the war, the airport was an adjunct of the McChord Air Force Base housing P-38 airplanes. The Port of Olympia was an extensive lend-lease port during the 1930s and was designated for air use when war was declared. With the outbreak of war, Prefabricated Ships Inc., later Puget Sound Shipbuilding and Olympia Shipbuilding, located at the port and in 1942 large quantities of lend-lease cargo went through Olympia bound for Russia.

After the war, Budd Inlet was home to a large fleet of reserve ships which anchored off Gull Harbor. The fleet reached its peak of 185 ships moored in Budd Inlet in 1960 and they were used for such purposes as grain storage until the early 1970s.

The decade ended with a visit of the Freedom Train and the eventual creation of Capitol Lake, visualized since the Wilder and White plans for the Capitol Grounds in the 1920s.

A giant earthquake in April 1949 damaged many historic structures including the Chambers Block, Mottman Building, and Kneeland Hotel, and sounded the death knell for the clock tower of the old capitol. The lantern on the new capitol dome was also severely damaged and had to be replaced with a lighter cap.

One of the high points of the depression-ridden year of 1933 was the visit of the historic frigate, the U.S.F. Constitution. Built in 1797, the ship was first used against French privateers and destroyed the English frigate Guerriere *in the War of 1812. Rebuilt a number number of times, the ship had been refurbished through the contributions of American schoolchildren in 1925 before its visit to Olympia.*

The Olympia community greeted and entertained the ship and crew in grand style during the ten-day stay of the ship. Band concerts, a grand naval ball, luncheons, and private parties feted the guests. Over 39,000 people visited the ship as it welcomed its four millionth visitor in Olympia. "Old Olympia" photo from the collection of Jeffers Studio

To publicize the visit of the U.S.S. Constitution, *the Olympia Chamber of Commerce issued $2,000 worth of "oyster money" to commemorate the visit and for use at local establishments, while defraying the costs of entertaining the crew of the* Constitution.

The wooden money, patterned after the famous Tenino wooden nickel issued in 1932 and 1933, was in the shape of an oyster shell with a drawing of the Constitution *on one side and the slogan "Dig the Canal" on the other.*

The canal was the Columbia River-Grays Harbor-Puget Sound Canal, which had long been a dream of area residents to join Puget Sound at its most southern tip at Budd Inlet with Grays Harbor and an inland route to the Columbia River. The idea by 1933 was not a new one. Indians for generations had canoed the waterway, which led from Black Lake to the Black River, thence to the Chehalis River and finally to Grays Harbor.

The "Dig the Canal" slogan was part of an effort to persuade the federal government to undertake the canal as a WPA project rather than the Grand Coulee Dam. From the State Capital Museum Collection

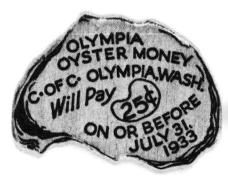

In the shadow of the capitol the hard-pressed people of the depression years held forth at "Little Hollywood" on the tide flats that were to become the well-groomed shores of the picturesque Capitol Lake. "Old Olympia" photo from the collection of Jeffers Studio

Another highlight of 1933 was the visit by the Anheuser-Busch Clydesdales here shown on State Street, north of City Hall. Notice the brick streets and streetcar tracks. "Old Olympia" photo from the Jeffers Studio Collection

By 1931 unemployment in Seattle had reached 60 percent and in other areas the figure was 23 percent. An Unemployed Citizen League formed in Seattle in 1931 and formed a self-aid group but by May 1932 the depression had deepened and relief was no longer available.

A coalition of various unemployed workers' leagues and councils decided to converge on Olympia in January 1933 to demonstrate their plight to the legislators and governor. Between 500 and 1,000 gathered in the old Capitol Building and a delegation marched on the capitol seeking unemployment insurance, cash payments, relief for rural families, and prohibition of foreclosures or tax sales. They also sought free water, light, and gas.

Greeted by locked doors, elevators, and highway patrolmen in the corridors, the group gathered outside with placards. Legislators did act to grant aid to the unemployed but the Republic of the Unemployed was not satisfied.

Again in March, they convened in Olympia to demand more taxes on the rich and such items as milk and hot lunches for their children. When the marchers arrived on March 1, a group called the "American Vigilantes of Thurston County" were there to greet them and directed them with broom handles to Priest Point Park, where they spent the night surrounded by over 800 vigilantes and policemen. They were ordered to leave the park the next day, but a few did get to see the governor. "Old Olympia" photo from the Jeffers Studio Collection

Governor Clarence Martin met with members of the Lummi Tribe in 1934 who had come to discuss fishing rights and the construction of Bonneville and Grand Coulee dams on the Columbia River.

After the Indians performed in Sylvester Park they met here in the old Capitol Building to present Governor Martin with a war bonnet and named him honorary chief, called **Pal-AwkTen**, ("Tall Male Cedar"). Jeffers Studio "Old Olympia" photo

John C. Percival was the son of pioneer Samuel Percival. Both of them were to become legendary in Olympia maritime history.

Percival was given charge of the dock in 1877 at the age of sixteen. From that date to 1936 he was agent for Goodall, Perkins & Co., and its successors, Pacific Coast Steamship Line, Pacific Steamships, and the Admiral Line, as well as the Oregon Railway and Navigation Company and the Northern Pacific. The family is commemorated in the Percival Landing City Park on Olympia's waterfront.

The interior of Percival's office is shown here laden with the history of the steamship era. Percival himself is presiding. "Old Olympia" photo from the Jeffers Studio Collection

Olympians were still traveling on brick streets in this 1943 photo of Washington Street, looking north from Fifth. On the right are the Jeffers Studio, Capitol Theater Building, and the Security Building. The Martin Building is at left. State Capitol Museum photo

Ted Maxin and his partner Walt Romaninski operated a Richfield station in Tumwater during the 1930s, at the site of the present Falls Terrace Restaurant. The station, along with some ninety other buildings, fell victim to the building of the freeway in the 1950s. State Capital Museum photo

The Foy Store at the corner of Pacific and Lacey streets was a Lacey landmark for many years. Built by Gordon Foy who had owned a store near the mill, the tile-roofed structure was built in 1925. The store offered a variety of goods including hay and feed, general merchandise, and drygoods, and had a barbershop, soda fountain, and gas station at various times in its history. Ann Foy, Mr. Foy's sister, was the postmistress in the combination store-post office for forty-eight years.

The Foys sold the store in the late 1930s to Henry C. Turner, who operated a grocery store, post office, and laundromat there for many years. Lacey Museum photo

The Tumwater Town Hall, housing the fire department, was built in 1935. State Capital Museum photo

One of the mainstays of Tumwater was O'Hare's Store which was located across from the present Falls Terrace Restaurant on the west side of Deschutes Way. The store was destroyed to make way for the freeway in the 1950s. State Capital Museum photo

Members of Tumwater pioneer Michael T. Simmons's family gathered in Tumwater for this portrait. Henderson House Museum photo

After KGY moved from the log cabin on St. Martin's campus to the Captial Park Building in 1932, the station was owned by Archie Taft who also owned KOL in Seattle.

In 1939 the station was purchased by Tom Olsen who in 1941 moved KGY to the Rockway-Leland Building at State and Washington streets. Specially designed, acoustically perfect studios housed the station with a 150-foot-tall tower on the roof of the building.

The station brought a number of live broadcasts, remote presentations, and local talent to its listeners from the studios. *KGY Radio photo*

The Clarence J. Lord House which is now the State Capital Museum was built in 1922 by Lord, a native of New York who became a banker in Olympia.

The house, designed by Joseph Wohleb, had thirty-two rooms and five fireplaces. Adjoining the main structure is the Coach House which housed Lord's prized automobiles. The home featured beautiful woods and fine workmanship, which have been retained in the museum.

Mr. Lord died in 1937 and his wife deeded the house to the state of Washington in 1939 in memory of her husband, to be used as a museum which has been open since 1942.

The musuem features displays on state and territorial history, Native American exhibits, and Olympia and Thurston County historical information. The house is on the National Register of Historic Places. State Capital Museum photo

Longshoremen at the Port of Olympia were kept busy loading phosphate, bound for the Orient in 1947. Over 300,000 tons of the commodity crossed port wharves that year. Port of Olympia photo

Country western music was in its heyday during those years before the rock 'n' roll of the 1950s. Oakie Armstrong and the U. E. Chamberlain Carboys were weekly performers at the Tropics Ballroom where KGY broadcast live.

KGY also unaugurated a unique drive-in broadcasting studio from Martin Way in 1948. On a glass-enclosed stage, the Oakie and his Carboys band held forth with a variety of local and national talent, broadcast over the station. Listeners could drive up to see the performers and hear them over KGY. Photo courtesy of Oakie Armstrong

This panoramic view of the port also shows the mothball fleet which came to the Olympia area and anchored off Gull Harbor. Port of Olympia photo

The Olympia Centennial was highlighted by a festive parade shown here on Main Street in 1950. This float featured some of the collection of the State Capital Historical Association formed in 1946, and a replica of the old wooden Capitol. Merle Junk photo from the Ron Allen Collection

1950-1970

The 1950s ushered in a new freeway which was dedicated in 1958 in the Capital Community. The construction of Interstate 5 permanently changed the topography of the area especially in Tumwater which lost ninety homes to the construction, but through a civic effort the historic Crosby House was saved.

The decade did lead off with a gala celebration for Olympia's centennial. A pioneer king and queen were crowned in Sylvester Park where a log cabin was headquarters for the festivities. A "Street of Yesterday" was constructed along Water Street and the "Olympia of Today and Tomorrow" was featured at the Armory. Carnivals, parades, dances, and "The Olympian Century," a pageant at Stevens field, were some of the other events.

The Korean War brought heavy warehousing and shipping of military cargo bound for the conflict from the Port of Olympia and an exodus of some ships from the mothball fleet at Gull Harbor. The remaining ships became a storehouse for sixteen and a half million bushels of wheat, beginning in 1953.

In the 1950s record amounts of lumber left port docks from area mills. In 1957, Olympia was second only to Coos Bay, Oregon, in exporting West Coast lumber that year.

Building was also under way when Penney's, Millers, and Goldberg's stores were built, all designed by Joseph Wohleb in the 1950s. The destructive earthquake of 1949 damaged a number of older downtown buildings so significantly that new buildings had to be put up in their place.

The earthquake also played havoc with the lantern atop the capitol dome. It had to be replaced with a lighter material to create more stability for the decorative piece. The General Administration Building and State Library were also built during the 1950s on the campus.

The completion of Capitol Lake by the damming of the Deschutes River added the reflection pool for the magnificent domed legislative building and a fine recreational attraction for Olympia as well. Deschutes Parkway around the lake has become a favorite jogging and bike path area.

In the fifties Sylvester Park became the center of controversy when the 1955 legislature passed an act which retracted the city's proprietary rights to the park. The state was planning to build an underground parking garage at the site.

Under the stalwart leadership of Margaret McKenny and others, the city enacted a protective ordinance for the park and also petitioned the preservation of the city's old watershed as a natural park near the city. Miss McKenny and her followers succeeded in preserving the unique area which has been made unto a one-and-a-half-mile hiking trail rich in native flora and fauna.

The Olympia School District was busy in 1956 with the completion of James Madison, John Rogers and Jefferson Junior High to accommodate the area's growing population. The North Thurston School District joined with South Bay in 1953 to form what is now the largest district in the area with over 8,000 students.

In 1957, residents got together to inaugurate "Lakefair," the capital's annual summer fest. Olympia had hosted a number of summer celebrations including an annual "Pagan Fest" but in 1956 hosted a carnival and in 1957 officially dubbed the celebration "Lakefair" which has grown steadily since that time with floats, sports events, concerts, arts and other festive events.

Few long-time Olympians will forget Friday, March 13, 1959, when fifteen runaway box cars traveled the two-mile 1% grade south of Olympia and slammed into the downtown area at Fourth and Adams streets, killing one and injuring scores of other people.

The 1960s were a time of great change in all three communities. In Tumwater, recently ravaged by the construction of the freeway, a bright spot was the newly completed Tyee Motor Inn, a luxury spot which was a favorite of legislators. Lacey was becoming the bedroom community with the development of Tanglewilde, a planned residential district.

The 1960s saw expansion on the Capitol Campus as it moved east of Capitol Way. When the Employment Security and Highways Licenses buildings were erected, a number of landmarks fell under the wrecking ball, including the Olympia High School and Maple Park Apartments.

In 1961 three new high schools were built in Olympia, Tumwater and Lacey. In Tumwater they were joined by the development at Southgate, capitalizing on the new freeway access. In Lacey, Georgia Pacific built a new mill and Weyerhaeuser constructed a facility at the old Union Mills site.

The Columbus Day storm hit the northwest on October 12, 1962, with seventy-eight-mile per hour winds which killed two people in the Olympia area and caused extensive damage to buildings and trees.

In 1963 a group of developers transformed the former Chambers family homestead and golf course

Another view of the Centennial parade, this time as it passed the Funk-Volland Building at Fifth and Main. Notice the costume-clad onlookers in the windows of the building. Merle Junk photo from the Ron Allen Collection

into the innovative retirement center of Panorama City.

Responding to this new population and the bustling suburban growth, Lacey was incorporated as a city in 1966 with Al Homann as its first mayor. Lacey's first shopping center, South Sound Center, opened also in 1966 and fittingly enough, the first city officers were sworn in there, representing the new trend of the community toward suburban shopping.

In Olympia, the picturesque city hall was left to the firemen and a new moat-encircled city hall was built in a Robert Wohleb design in 1966.

The era of smokestacks and plywood mills drew to a close when Simpson, Georgia Pacific, and St. Regis mills closed, victims of changing markets. The landmark Mottman's Store also closed its doors in 1967 after nearly a century of mercantile familiarity in Olympia.

A new era began at the close of the sixties when The Evergreen State College was authorized by the state legislature on Cooper Point, the site of the historic Athens University. The institution has changed and enlivened the Capital Community's cultural and social climate.

The Olympia Brewery brought its own Clydesdale team and wagon out for a display at the Olympia Centennial. Henderson House Museum photo

Stores participated in the Centennial events as well. Here Miller's displayed the wedding gown worn by Mrs. T. I. McKenny in its window and also featured live models during part of the exhibit. State Capital Museum photo

Almost everyone got into the spirit of the 1950 Centennial. Shown here are county workers outside the Thurston County Courthouse dressed in their pioneer best for the occasion. State Capital Museum photo

No one who lived in Olympia or indeed in the entire Northwest in 1949 will forget April 13 of that year. An earthquake registering eight in intensity struck just before noon, killing two people in Olympia and eight elsewhere in the Northwest. The quake struck with such force that it shook the buildings in Olympia—many of which could not be salvaged. The result was that many of the landmark structures of downtown had to be torn down and replaced with newer buildings.

The Governor Hotel and the Elks Building are shown here on Capitol Way.

One person was killed by falling brick at the Washington Veneer Plant at the port fill shown here.

Margaret McKenny was the daughter of pioneer T. I. McKenny and she went on to become Olympia's most outspoken advocate of conservation of nature and defender of wilderness.

Miss McKenny studied at the Lawthrop School of Landscape Architecture in Groton, Massachusetts and practiced as a landscape architect. However, her true love was the wild. An author of more than fifteen books, she was an authority on wild mushrooms and wildflowers and a founder of the Olympia Audubon Society. She led the fight to retain the Nisqually Delta as a natural preserve and helped keep the old Olympia Watershed as a wilderness area. She received a national conservation award in 1966 and in 1967 a site in the Capitol Forest was dedicated to her.

She is pictured here with the many schoolchildren she loved as she taught them about nature. She died in 1969. *State Capital Museum photo*

The Tivoli Fountain on the Capitol Campus, which was installed in 1953, is a brass replica of one of the fountains in the Tivoli Gardens in Copenhagen. The idea of local businessman Peter Schmidt, it was a gift of the Olympia-Tumwater Foundation. *Norman Gallacci photo*

Olympians celebrated a frightening Friday the thirteenth in March 1959 when fifteen railroad cars went on a runaway rampage into downtown Olympia. Photo from the Daily Olympian

KGY constructed a new station at the foot of North Washington Street overlooking Budd Inlet in 1960. It was one of the most uniquely situated stations in the country. KGY photo

The new Olympia High School, properly known as the William Winlock Miller High School, as were its predecessors, is located on the former Cloverfields Farm owned by Gen. Hazard Stevens. Pendleton Miller, grandson of the original William Winlock Miller, arranged for a reversionary clause in land transactions so the family could again donate land for the school. The school was built on a campus format encompassing nine buildings. Although the industrial arts building was completed in 1957, the school itself was not dedicated until 1961.

In the background are Hazard Lake and the many houses in the area. Merle Junk photo from the Ron Allen Collection

The spectre of the H-bomb loomed over Olympia in 1961 when a family stayed in a fallout shelter for one week in Olympia. Radio KGY broadcast live from the shelter bringing the reality of nuclear attack to the ears of local listeners. Merle Junk photo

A furious pace of construction was under way in the early 1960s when the capitol moved east of Capitol Way. The Highways-Licenses Building shown at right was one of the first completed. Del Ogden photo

A number of familiar Olympia landmarks fell to the wrecking ball with the expansion of the Capitol Grounds. The Capital Apartments are being razed here. Del Ogden photo

Tumwater Falls Park, located on the site of the original town of Tumwater and later the Hazard Stevens Elk Farm, is a beautiful haven with its pathways along unique waterfalls and plantings. The park was completed in 1963 and welcomes thousands of freeway-weary travelers yearly in Tumwater.

The park's visitor center has a map showing the locations of historic sites along the falls and also boasts an Indian petroglyph brought to the site from Harstene Island.

The Deschutes River salmon run was constructed along the falls in 1952 by the Washington Department of Fisheries, and holding pens constructed in 1961 aid in counting, measuring, and cultivating the thousands of fish which travel upstream yearly. Del Ogden photo

Governor Rosellini cuts the ribbon, opening the new Capital Savings Bank at Fifth and Franklin in Olympia in 1964. Merle Junk photo from the Ron Allen Collection

The St. Martin's College Pavilion in Lacey, completed in 1966, is home to a number of sporting and community events. Up to 6,000 persons can be seated for conventions, 5,000 for basketball and other sporting events, and 2,500 for banquets. Norman Gallacci photo

Anna Blom was the proprietor of a used book store in Olympia for over forty years. Mrs. Blom was born in Russia and came to the United States as a young woman. Her bookstore at 522 S. Washington in the Reed Block was a treasure trove of ancient tomes. Mrs. Blom died in 1972. Del Ogden photo

The Olympia City Hall was completed in 1966 when city government moved from the historic site downtown. The uniquely styled round structure boasted a moat complete with goldfish when it was completed, which has since been filled in. The Plum Street structure was designed by architect Robert Wohleb, the son of Joseph Wohleb. Norman Gallacci photo

Sunset Life Insurance Company began its operations in 1937 from a building in downtown Olympia. In 1959 this building was completed as the Home Office of Sunset Life Insurance at the site of the former Fred Carlyon home. An addition was completed to the main structure in 1980.

Sunset Life is represented by over 1,000 sales representatives in thirteen western states and Germany. It has over $1.5 billion of life insurance in force and is rated A+ by Best's Insurance Reports. The home office employs approximately 150 men and women, primarily from the Olympia-Lacey-Tumwater area. Merle Junk photo from the Ron Allen Collection

Christmas Island was built in 1959 by engineers at Ft. Lewis. Volunteers and members of the Olympia Chamber of Commerce assisted in the construction and decoration. Leonard Huber of Seattle created the nativity scene.

The Christmas Island idea has been a part of Olympia's Christmas, lighting up Capitol Lake since that date. Merle Junk photo from the Ron Allen Collection

The Pet Parade in Olympia has long been the capping event of summer in the lives of Olympia area children. The parade began as a 4-H club event in conjunction with the "Paga Festival," a forerunner of Lakefair in 1929. By 1932, it was being called the "Pet and Doll Parade" and children were treated to an afternoon matinee after the pageant. In 1939 the Olympian *took over sponsorship for the event, which has grown to grand proportions, allowing children to show their favorite pets, dress up imaginatively, and enjoy a movie and ice cream with it all. Merle Junk photo from the Ron Allen Collection*

The Panorama City facility, now over twenty years old, encompasses 150 acres and accommodates 1,200 adult residents. The total-life-care environment offers a variety of living arrangements including single family, duplex, multiplex, and apartment living, as well as a 106-bed convalescent and rehabilitative care complex.

Vista Village, an adult condominium community, is also located in Lacey. Norman Gallacci photo

An earthquake which struck on April 29, 1965, caused considerable damage as it registered 6.5 on the Richter scale. The downtown suffered minor damage and the Legislative Building at the Capitol had to be refurbished to bind all parts of the structure together after the quake. Del Ogden photo

Fourth Avenue is shown looking east circa 1964. Del Ogden photo

Herb Anderson of radio KGY was the master of ceremonies when South Sound Center officially opened in 1966, here in front of the Sears store. The shopping center changed the character of Lacey, and fittingly enough, the ceremonies swearing in the new officers of the recently incorporated City of Lacey were held at the mall. KGY also had a broadcast studio at the mall for a time. KGY photo

South Sound Center was developed by Bob Blume of Lacey and features nine major stores and over ninety stores and specialty shops. A variety of displays and programs are presented at the mall throughout the year, including art shows, boat exhibits, energy fairs, antique shows, boat expositions, garden fairs, and civic displays. Del Ogden photo

The interior of South Sound Mall seen here reflects the "main street" character of malls as residents meet and interact with one another. Del Ogden photo

The Olympia Federal Savings Building at Capitol and Fifth in downtown Olympia was completed in 1967 in a design by architect Stacey Bennett.

Olympia Federal began in 1906 to encourage savings and aid in home ownership. First directors were C. H. Springer, Millard Lemon, C. J. Lord, P. M. Troy, George E. Filley, and James McDowell. The institution has served the Capital Community well, now boasting over $118 million in assets with branch in West Olympia, Tumwater, Lacey, and Belfair. Del Ogden photo

The Evergreen State College was authorized by the state legislature in 1967 to be the newest and most innovative of the state's four-year institutions. Del Odgen photo

Lakefair, which began with a carnival in 1956, grew throughout the 1950s and 1960s to include parades, floats, the Governor's Festival of the Arts, a treasure hunt, and fireworks.

Shown here is the annual coronation of the Lakefair queen from among princesses representing local high schools. The event held at Capitol Lake always features a unique announcement from air, sea, or land of the new princess. The Capitalarians, the active civic group who make Lakefair a reality each year, escort the ladies. KGY photo

Changes in demand and shipping regulations substantially changed the character of the Port of Olympia during the 1960s when it became a major log shipping port. Port of Olympia photo

In the years between 1966 and 1968, the Port of Olympia quadrupled its total tonnage with 97 percent more shipping in 1968 than any previous year. The port was shipping 9.9 percent of all Washington and Oregon log exports in 1968.

The busy waterfront was engulfed in logs. Port of Olympia photo

The Capital Community had been bisected by the new freeway by the end of the 1960s and was dotted with new shopping areas befitting the mobility of the freeway-driving society. Here the view is northward from Tumwater showing Capitol Lake, the freeway, and the Reserve Fleet at a distance. Port of Olympia photo

1970-1985

The 1970s brought many changes to the Capital Community as the national trend of shopping centers and suburban development continued to affect the three communities.

St. Peter Hospital constructed a new building in 1971; other new edifices in Olympia included the Bank of Olympia at Eighth and Capitol Way, the Evergreen Plaza Building at 711 South Capitol Way, and a new *Olympian* building on East State Street, all built in 1972.

The last of the reserve ships of the World War II mothball fleet left Gull Harbor in 1972. Opening in April 1972, The Evergreen State College created new cultural and educational horizons for Olympia bringing as it did a unique philosophy implemented by outstanding instructors. The campus, too, was original: its architecture sought to blend with the natural beauty of the Cooper Point environs. The college is located near the proposed site of the People's University, planned but never built in the early 1900s.

In Lacey during the early 1970s more and more shopping areas were developed to keep pace with its phenomenal residential growth as a bedroom community to Olympia. In 1973 Lacey community leaders organized the International Music Arts and Dance Festival. Also in Lacey, St. Martin's High School closed it doors in the mid-1970s.

The community celebrated the United States Bicentennial by gathering in Sylvester Park for an old-fashioned Fourth of July, complete with an oration given in the new gazebo constructed by Patrons of South Sound Cultural Activities (POSSCA). Area children also collected historical materials and a North Thurston District high school class put a marker along Interstate 5 near the site of the Medicine Creek Treaty of 1854.

In 1977, the Olympia area was named one of the fastest-growing areas in the United States. That same year the county government moved from the cramped quarters of the historic sandstone Thurston County Courthouse on Capitol Way to a new complex atop Mottman Hill overlooking Capitol Lake and Puget Sound.

After a long effort to acquire a new library, the Olympia Timberland Library opened in 1978 on the historic Ostrander Block in Olympia. Citizens of Olympia had passed a 1976 Bicentennial bond issue of $1.5 million to build the new facility. Branches of the Timberland Regional Library System are also located in Lacey and Tumwater.

The West Side of Olympia also began to bloom in the late 1970s. The growth of this area, fostered by The Evergreen State College, culminated in the opening of the Capital Mall in 1978. A number of other West Side shopping districts have been developed as well in the area once known as Marshville.

Once the symbol of community prosperity, the smokestacks of the lumber mills on the port fill came down in the early 1970s to make room for the burgeoning log traffic. The decline in lumber milling made the stacks obsolete. Del Ogden photo

The development of the malls and outlying shopping districts has created a renewed commitment to the downtown area of Olympia. The Rural/Urban Design Assistance Team (R/UDAT) of the American Institute of Architects visited Olympia in 1979 and in 1990. Their recommendations along with a healthy downtown association of merchants have revitalized the business district.

The 1980s brought renewed interest in protecting historic structures. The City of Olympia inaugurated a wide-ranging historic preservation program to provide interpretative markers to Historic Register properties and to administer an incentive program for rehabilitation of historic structures.

The Capital Community continues to celebrate with a bigger and more entertaining Lakefair in July each year. The popular Labor Day waterfront celebration "Harbor Days," begun in 1974, features picturesque tugboats

The Evergreen State College was dedicated in April 1971. The college is uniquely located on 1,000 acres of forested timberland, including 3,300 feet of waterfront on Eld Inlet, a waterway of Puget Sound. The newest four-year college in Washington, Evergreen is noted for its innovative concept of interdisciplinary studies, independent study, and internship programs as well as its commentary grading system. Over 6,200 graduates of the school speak well of its program and it has been acclaimed by national publications for its excellent approach to learning. Norman Gallacci photo

which vie for prizes as they churn the waters of Budd Inlet.

Olympia was part of the fitness craze and won fame as the site of the first Women's Olympic Marathon Trials in May 1984.

In Tumwater, the city created the Henderson House Museum in 1978 and a historical park in the area where small mills once lined the Deschutes River. The well-manicured grounds and play areas belie the bustle that was once the "Lowell of the Pacific" of Tumwater. The Henderson House Museum is located in the restored Naumann House on Deschutes Way.

Lacey also opened a museum in an effort to recollect its past days of racetrack glory and beginnings of what is now a large suburban community. The museum was created in the first Lacey City Hall and fire station, originally the Russell House. A first phase of a new city hall was built in 1979.

Each of the communities of Olympia, Lacey, and Tumwater retains its unique identity and although they are geographically inseparable, each contributes it special ambience to the Capital Community.

In Tumwater, Washington's first community, residents have rallied to recognize its status and have undertaken the creation of a museum and historical park in the area where small mills once lined the Deschutes River. The well-manicured grounds and play areas belie the bustle that was once the "Lowell of the Pacific" of Tumwater. The Henderson House Museum located in a restored home is awash in historic photographs of Tumwater and boasts an avid volunteer corps dedicated to preserving its history. The park is a favorite gathering spot for young and old alike.

Lacey, too, has opened a museum in an effort to recollect its past days of racetrack glory and the beginnings of what is now a large suburban community. A new city hall was built in 1979 and a new police station is planned for the wooded area near St. Martin's. The college has also adapted to the age of the eighties adding an impressive computer curriculum in an effort to meet the age head-on.

Each of the communities of Olympia, Lacey, and Tumwater retains its unique identity and although they are geographically inseparable, each contributes its special ambience to the Capital Community as it looks forward to the challenges of the 1980s and beyond.

Fire destroyed all but thirty units of the Tyee Motor Inn on January 26, 1970 in a conflagration which sent visiting legislators and lobbyists scurrying. A new facility soon rose from the ashes. Del Ogden photo

The new Tyee was completed in stages in the early 1970s and is now owned by Vance Hotels. Norman Gallacci photo

The Lacey Music Arts and Dance Festival premiered in 1973 as a Chamber of Commerce activity to enliven the summer. First known as the International Music Arts and Dance Festival, the event attracted 30,000 people the first year. In 1974 the Miss Thurston County Pageant became part of the festivities. The event has been held at various locations in Lacey including St. Martin's Pavilion and South Sound Center.

In recent years themes have varied for the event, now known as MAD-FEST, ranging from a mountain men encampment and firemen's muster to talent competitions and an art show.

Some of the participants in the 1974 event are shown here. Lacey Museum photo

South Puget Sound Community College, formerly Olympia Technical Community College, was founded in 1963 as part of the Olympia School District where it was housed in the old Montgomery Ward Building. Since 1970 it has been a part of the state community college system, offering college transfer, occupational, continuing education, and leisure education courses. Serving approximately 9,000 students each year, SPSCC is the largest higher education institution in Thurston County. The beautiful, wooded campus is located at 2011 Mottman Road and encompasses an eighty-five-acre area. As partners in Community College District Twelve, SPSCC and Centralia College together serve Thurston and Lewis counties. Norman Gallacci photo

In 1977 the work experience class of Olympia High School built a 1.5-mile walking trail through Olympia's old watershed, forming Watershed Park. The trail is named to honor long-time city manager G. Eldon Marshall.

The city used the site, known historically as Moxlie Creek, and surrounding artesian wells as a water source from 1913 to the late 1930s when they moved the operation to McAllister Springs full-time in 1949. In an advisory ballot in 1955, the pristine woodland was saved from development and the scene was set for the enjoyment of this urban wilderness. Norman Gallacci photo

Percival Landing Park on Olympia's waterfront was completed in 1977 and was constructed at the site of the famous steamship wharf run by the Percival family.

The whale was carved by Olympia artist Joe Tougas, who duplicated his work for Yashiro, Japan, Olympia's sister city, in 1981. Norman Gallacci photo

The Thurston County Courthouse, completed in 1977, is the latest in a long line of courthouses for Thurston County, all located in Olympia since 1861 when the county seat was voted to Olympia from Tumwater. The three-building complex is located atop Mottman hill overlooking Capitol Lake and the city of Olympia. Norman Gallacci photo

Capital Mall opened in October 1978 on the west side of Olympia with forty-five stores under one roof on its sixty-five-acre site. That number has increased to 102 tenants and spurred the growth of a number of satellite shopping areas adjacent to the mall. Norman Gallacci photo

The Olympia Library, which was dedicated in 1978, is a bustling center of activity in downtown Olympia.

Captain D. B. Finch established a free public reading room at Fourth and Columbia in Olympia in 1869 and Olympians had been able to use the Territorial Library purchased by Isaac Stevens in 1853 which was housed in Olympia. In 1896 the Women's Club started library service on the fourth Saturday of each month and in 1909 the city took over the maintenance of the public library. In 1914 the city completed its own Carnegie Library at Seventh and Franklin through a $25,000 gift from the Carnegie Foundation. Olympia joined a regional library system in 1948, and in 1968 formed the Timberland Regional Library. In 1976 a Bicentennial bond issue of $1.5 million enabled the construction of the present facility at Eighth and Franklin. Norman Gallacci photo

Lacey built the first phase of a new city hall in 1979 among the towering trees near St. Martin's College and left its former quarters to house a city museum. Norman Gallacci photo

The Lacey Museum, a restored farmhouse of 1928 vintage, served as Lacey Fire Department, police station, and city hall before being moved and renovated for museum use.

The museum was opened in 1981 and features displays of local history. Norman Gallaci photo

Olympia's annual summer festival, Lakefair, lights up the summer with fun. The annual parade first egun in 1959 became the grand twilight parade in 1963 attracting hundreds of entries, from spectacular floats to child-pleasing clowns.

A highlight of the year's events is the announcing of the new Lakefair queen, which is accomplished in novel ways each year; everything from hot air balloons to firecrackers.

The festival is capped by a spectacular display of fireworks which light up the sky over Capitol Lake.

Buttons are sold each year to help finance the many activities. A series of buttons featuring the historical buildings and landmarks within the three cities of Olympia, Tumwater, and Lacey focusing on the state capitol campus structures and culminating in the Territorial State capitol in 1989 was a highlight of the button series. *Photo by Del Ogden*

Each year a carnival settles around Capitol Lake Park for Lakefair week, ending the second weekend in July. Photo courtesy of the Olympia Chamber of Commerce

Another favorite activity of Lakefair is the yearly visit of a naval vessel, either from the U.S. or Canadian navies, which draws large crowds of visitors to port docks. Del Ogden photo

The latest incarnation of the Farmers Market began in Olympia in 1973 as a project of the Retired Senior Volunteer Program to promote good nutrition for seniors and to help finance RSVP activities. With the aid of VISTA workers who first set up the market on the shores of Capitol Lake, the project grew, doubling its size each year. In 1975 the market moved to its Plum Street site for an eight-year tenure. The market moved to a site at Capitol Way and Thurston Streets in the 1980s. Norman Gallacci photo

The Henderson House Museum, located in Tumwater, houses hundreds of photographs of early Tumwater, the Olympia Brewery, logging, and the original Tumwater Post Office. Since its opening in 1981, the museum has played host to thousands of visitors.

The early twentieth century home was restored by the city of Tumwater as one of the few remaining homes within the Tumwater Historical District. The house adjoins the historic Crosby House, also owned by the city as part of the National Register of Historic Places site. Norman Gallaci photo

Tumwater Historical Park encompasses the northern end of the original village of Tumwater and now offers picnicking, nature walks, and a play area for younger visitors. Opened in July 1982, the park is part of the natural open space area which now reaches from downtown Olympia and Capitol Lake to the falls of the Deschutes River at Tumwater Falls Park. Norman Gallacci photo

The Capitol Lake Interpretive Center is the newest link in the Capitol Lake greenbelt. The center seeks to explain the complex biological system that is Capitol Lake while providing a unique nature experience, walking through its grounds. Norman Gallacci photo

The Olympia Isle Marina is the first stage of the extensive East Bay project of the Port of Olympia.

Planned are an 1,100-slip marina to be built in stages, twenty-four more acres of cargo yard, a commercial office building, housing for transient moorage, and launching facilities, all complemented by landscaping in miniparks and presented along a public esplanade. Initial dredging and filling were accomplished in 1982, creating fifty-four new acres of land. Norman Gallacci photo

Like the rest of the country, the Capital Community has joined the fitness game. The Olympia Rainrunners, a local club, has been at the forefront of organizing fun runs and other events which have become popular for young and old. Pictured here is the start of the Lakefair Run staged each July in conjunction with the fesival. Photo courtesy of the Olympia Chamber of Commerce

Thurston County residents turned out in force on Saturday May 12, 1984 when the first U.S. Women's Marathon Trials were staged in the Capital Community. Over 50,000 people watched a field of 238 runners vying for three positions on the U.S. Olympic team. Local running enthusiasts had gained the trials for Olympia by giving a professional and committed presentation to Olympic Committee members. Olympia's Capital City Marathon, run on nearly the same course, had proved to be exceptionally successful prior to the selection.

Seen here at the start of the race are women runners led by Julie Brown at the far right, who won second place. Olympian *photo by Steve Bloom*

Joan Benoit won the first U.S. Women's Olympic Marathon Trials with a time of two hours, thirty-one minutes, and four seconds, and is shown here at the finish line wearing her crown and lei furnished by Dole Pineapple, primary sponsor of the event. Benoit had been a pre-race favorite but had undergone knee surgery just seventeen days before the event. She was followed by Julie Brown in second place and Julie Isphording in third place.

The trials were a community effort by hundreds of volunteers who coordinated almost every phase of the run. All qualifiers were flown to Olympia, housed, fed, and entertained free of charge through corporate and community contributions. Olympian *photo by Dick Milligan*

"Harbor Days," which is celebrated yearly on Labor Day weekend, began in 1974 emphasizing tugboat races which by 1983 had grown to twenty-five tugs and an arts and crafts fair and other seagoing craft competitions, as well as a fly-over of antique aircraft. The events were first held at the Port of Olympia, but have been moved in recent years to the Percival Landing Park.

Other waterfront activities promoted in recent years include the Wooden Boat Festival with classic vessels, a regatta and races, and the Black Lake Regatta, a hydroplane event.

Shown here is some of the action of the tugboat races on Budd Inlet. Photo by Scott Schoch, courtesy of Pat Haskett

Columbia Capital Medical Center which opened in 1985 as the Black Hills Community Hospital has grown to become a 110-bed, full service hospital which includes a cancer treatment center, diabetes wellness center, birthing suite area, ambulatory center, and medical office building.

In 1995 the hospital added a new 16,000-square-foot centralized outpatient addition and was acquired by Columbia/HCA. The hospital serves Southwest Washington. Photograph by Owen and Owen Photography courtesy of Columbia Capital Medical Center

The Washington Center celebrated its tenth anniversary in 1995. The theater has welcomed nearly 800,000 people since its opening in 1985. Built at the site of the old Olympic Theater, the facility features a 987-seat Mainstage Theater and a Stage II "Black Box" Theater accommodating 125 patrons. As part of the Phase III capitol campaign the historic Wurlitzer organ installed in 1924 as part of the historic Liberty Theater at this location was restored to the Center in 1995. Photograph by Steve Vento, courtesy of the Washington Center for the Performing Arts

One of Olympia's most historic and picturesque spots, Sylvester Park, continues to be a favorite gathering place for the community, a bower of greenery in the summer, a cascade of leaves in the fall, and a charming resting spot in the spring. Norman Gallaci photo

The waterfront village of Olympia is portrayed in this 1871 painting by Elizabeth Kimball. The wife of a Tumwater minister, Mrs. Kimball lived in the area only briefly and then returned to her East Coast home. But she left a charming portrait of nineteenth-century Olympia. Carved out of the tall pines at the southern tip of Puget Sound, the village was in a superb setting of the magnificent Olympic Mountains and the ever-changing Puget Sound. From the State Capital Museum Collection

The Olympia Center was completed in 1986 on Capitol Way. The 48,000-square-foot facility operates as a community and senior center offering meeting space, food service, and recreational facilities for all ages. Photograph courtesy of City of Olympia Parks Department

The annual Lakefair fireworks display lights up the sky over the Capitol Grounds and presents a spectacular sight contrasted to the magnificent dome.

The Capital Community owes much of its history to state government, and many residents work for state government, so in a large sense our lives are lit by the dome and we stand in the shadow of its presence. Photo courtesy of the Olympia Chamber of Commerce

The New Market Vocational Skills Center is a ten-school district cooperative which offers students an extension of their home high school. The center provides vocational skills in fifteen different programs from cosmetology to collision repair. The facility, which is in its tenth year of operation, serves some 850 students from its Tumwater location. Photograph courtesy of New Market Vocational Skills Center

1985-1995

The years of 1985 to 1995 in the Olympia, Lacey, and Tumwater area have seen celebrations of milestones and looking back at the accomplishments of the past. Olympia was at the center of Washington State's gala 100th birthday in 1989 when Washingtonians gathered from around the state on the Capitol Campus for a series of events capped by the ceremonies on November 11, 1989, Statehood Day. Tumwater, "Washington's First Community," celebrated its sesquicentennial in 1995 with appropriate fanfare. Lacey will celebrate its 30th year of incorporation in 1996.

These years have also been marked with a new appreciation of our history and historic structures. The 1930s era Thurston County Courthouse, the Old Olympia Firehouse and City Hall, Lincoln School and the Bigelow House have all been renovated and preserved for future generations to enjoy. Active historic preservation groups are at work in Olympia, Lacey, and Tumwater.

Significant new public structures have gone up in all three communities. Lacey and Tumwater re-established city centers with new city halls and libraries while Olympia constructed a new central fire station.

The Capitol Campus, where new memorials were installed in 1987 and 1993, is the venue for the solemn commemoration of the sacrifices and contributions of Vietnam and Korean War veterans. As the need for state offices expanded, new headquarters buildings were constructed for the Department of Labor and Industries in Tumwater, the Department of Ecology in Lacey, and the Natural Resources Building on the East Capitol Campus in Olympia.

As the population of Olympia, Lacey, and Tumwater has increased to nearly 74,000, all three cities have added to their parklands to provide open space and recreational opportunities in both neighborhood and larger multi-use facilities. The completion of the third phase of the Percival Landing boardwalk in the City of Olympia in 1988 has opened up the waterfront to thousands of visitors and provided an excellent location for annual Harbor Days and Wooden Boat Fair celebrations. In Tumwater, the new Pioneer Park provides waterfront access along the Deschutes River. Parks on Hicks Lake and Long Lake in Lacey provide opportunities for lakefront recreation.

New schools and educational opportunities have sprung up to meet the needs of a new generation. Garfield and Roosevelt Schools in Olympia were razed for new facilities while Lincoln School, a 1920s Mission Revival landmark was preserved. New public schools were dedicated in all three cities. The New Market Skills Center was created to fill the need for vocational training in the area.

St. Martin's College in Lacey added the new Worthington Center to the campus in 1992 and celebrated its 100th anniversary in 1995.

Located on Percival Landing, "The Kiss" is a popular part of the City of Olympia's public art program. The cast aluminum life-size figures are the work of artist Richard S. Beyer. The artwork, which is owned by the City of Olympia, was commissioned by the Patrons of South Sound Cultural Activities (POSSCA) and was dedicated July 6, 1990. Photograph courtesy of the Olympia Parks Department

Area residents also enjoyed the lighter side of life with the many public art projects such as the fanciful sculpture, "The Kiss," on the Olympia's waterfront and "Sharing" the poignant sculpture at the Lacey Library. Over the past ten years, the Washington Center for the Performing Arts has proven to be a popular cultural focus, bringing fine entertainment to the area. The State Capital Museum, now a branch of the Washington State Historical Society, reopened in 1995 with refurbished facilities in the Lord Mansion and Coach House. The development of the East Bay Marina and revitalization of the Olympia waterfront have added to the enjoyment of mariners and landlubbers alike. Brewpubs and coffeehouses, the gath-

Centennial Station in Lacey along Yelm Highway was completed in 1992 after a five-year effort of volunteers. The 2700-square-foot station was dedicated on October 3, 1992, as the Amtrak Depot. Commemorative engraved bricks front the traditional style building which cost $350,000. Photograph courtesy of Buck Harmon who is pictured at the microphone.

ering spots of the '90s have added their ambience to a vibrant Olympia downtown. Lacey has grown with an office and commercial center along Sixth Avenue where a new transit center is also located. Festivals such as Evergreen's Super Saturday, the Tumwater Fourth of July Parade, and the Capital Food and Wine Festival at St. Martin's have joined the longtime community celebrations such as Lakefair as annual events.

As the new century approaches, new projects and events are planned. Olympia's new Farmer's Market on the Port peninsula opened its doors in April 1996. A spectacular new fountain, part of the Heritage Park project between Capitol Lake and Puget Sound was dedicated in May 1996. Lacey has extended its borders to Puget Sound at Nisqually Reach where the Hawk's Prairie Planned Community development will take shape. The City of Olympia will commemorate its 150th anniversary as the new century begins in the year 2000. With the new millennium will come more changes and challenges to the capital community, shaping and reshaping our hometowns.

The City of Olympia, which boasts the oldest fire department in the state, built a new central fire station on the east side of the city in 1992. The building was funded by a special city levy in 1988. Mounted outside the station is the historic firebell which was atop the former downtown firestation. The bell was purchased by the city in 1889 from McShane Bell Foundry of Baltimore. It weighs over 1,500 pounds and cost $256.53 when it was purchased. Photograph courtesy of the City of Olympia

Opposite page: Located in Tumwater, the Department of Labor and Industries Headquarters Building was completed in 1992. The distinctive design of the building with its multi-story entry atrium has drawn national attention to the 339,000-square-foot structure. This facility joins new state headquarters for the Department of Ecology in Lacey and the Natural Resources Building on the East Capitol Campus. Photograph courtesy of the Department of Labor and Industries

Located on Henderson Boulevard, Pioneer Park is Tumwater's largest park, covering eighty-five acres. The facility, purchased in 1987, features trails with access to the Deschutes River, a soccer field, and a softball field as well as natural and interpretative areas. The first phase of park development was completed in 1994. Photograph courtesy of Tumwater Parks Department

The Longhouse Education and Cultural Center at the Evergreen State College opened September 22, 1995. The 10,000-square-foot building was designed by Seattle architect Johnpaul Jones, of Choctaw-Cherokee heritage, with the advice of a planning committee. The structure reflects the traditional buildings of the Coastal Salish Native Americans. Features include wooden columns, a traditional round fire pit hearth, and hand-hewn cedar planks. Artwork for the structure is also in the Coastal Salish style. The ten-foot carved thunderbird at the entrance was made by Skokomish artist Andy Wilbur and Greg Colfax of the Makah Tribe. The structure is used for academic programs and cultural events with regional Native American communities. Photograph courtesy of the Evergreen State College

Completed in 1988, Percival Landing West was the last of three phases of construction of a public boardwalk and access to Olympia's waterfront. The landing extends from the Port of Olympia on the north to the Fourth Street bridge on the west. As part of the development, historical kiosks were placed along the walkway which describe the fascinating history of the city's waterfront. Photograph courtesy of Morton Safford James III, AIA Architects

Prominently located on the Washington State Capitol Campus, the Washington State Vietnam Veterans Memorial was dedicated May 25, 1987. The circular wall is engraved with the more than 1000 names of Washington residents who gave their lives or remain missing in action from 1963 to 1975 in the Vietnam War. The cost of erecting the memorial was raised entirely through private contributions. Photograph by Steve Borst courtesy of Washington State General Administration

The South Sound Maritime Heritage Association with the City of Olympia and the Port of Olympia annually sponsor "Harbor Days," a community festival celebrating the area's marine heritage. Staged at Olympia's Percival Landing and East Bay Marina, Harbor Days includes arts and crafts, food, and entertainment. Highlights of the three-day festival which was begun in 1974 are the show and race of vintage and modern tugboats. Photograph courtesy of CM3 Associates

With the construction of its new landmark City Hall in 1988, Tumwater has re-established its city center along Israel Road. Designed by BJSS Group, the City Hall is reminiscent of the historic landmark brewhouse built along the Deschutes River in 1906 by the Olympia Brewing Company. Photograph courtesy of BJSS Group, Architecture and Technology

The historic Bigelow House is Olympia's oldest home and one of the oldest frame houses still standing in the Northwest. It was built circa 1860 in the Gothic Revival style by pioneers Daniel R. Bigelow and his wife, Ann Elizabeth White Bigelow. He was an important figure in the separation of Washington from Oregon Territory; she was one of the region's first schoolteachers.

In 1994 the house was purchased from the Bigelow family by the non-profit Bigelow House Preservation Association. The following year, using a grant from the State of Washington, BHPA restored the house as closely as possible to the way it appeared in Washington's Territorial days. The renovated Bigelow House, containing an impressive collection of original furnishings and artifacts, opened to the public in 1995 on a limited basis. Photograph courtesy of the Bigelow House Preservation Association.

Bottom Right: Continuing to meet the challenges of providing cost effective and specialized health care, Providence St. Peter Hospital has expanded its facilities to include a chemical dependency center, a new professional building and a comprehensive outpatient and rehabilitation center. Sunshine House, which provides low cost accommodation for families of patients, was built in 1988 through the efforts of the Altrusa Club of Olympia and other donors. The Sisters of Providence built the Mother Joseph Care Center adjacent to the hospital in 1991.

The medical center provides regional specialty services including open heart surgery, diagnostic imaging, diabetes care, laser surgery applications, kidney dialysis, and a nationally accredited cancer care program. New specialized centers for psychiatric intensive care, and maternity have been added to the hospital. In 1991 St. Peter initiated a family practice residency program affiliated with the University of Washington Medical School.

Following the mission of the Sisters of Providence, the hospital serves low income families through the Family Practice Residency Program and Perinatal Care Clinic. Other community care includes the Sojourner Clinic for the homeless in downtown Olympia and the Community Dental Program. The St. Peter Health Foundation through its annual Christmas Forest and biannual "Hospital Happening" raises much of the funds for charity care. Shown is the specialized service building constructed in 1992. Photograph by Gant W. Eichrodt, courtesy of Providence St. Peter Hospital

The City of Lacey completed the addition to their City Hall in August of 1995. The addition features new City Council Chambers and room for City offices. Photograph courtesy of the City of Lacey

The dredging of the East Bay in 1982 created a moorage basin. Opened in 1983, East Bay Marina accommodates up to 488 boats ranging from twenty to forty-four feet. A public pedestrian trail connects East Bay Drive with the Port's marina parkway.

Beginning in 1982, the Port embarked on a modernization program for their facilities and systems. The Port was recognized in 1987 with the National "E" award for excellence in exports and was honored as the "Port of the Year" in 1987 by the Washington Public Ports Association. The Port garnered the Washington State Governor's Export Award in 1988. Among the Port's new facilities are a transit warehouse, rebuilt berths, and restored railroad service. The Port has also made substantial environmental improvements on its property such as paving and storm water systems. Shown here is a 1992 aerial view of the Port at low tide. Washington State Department of Transportation photograph courtesy of the Port of Olympia

Washington celebrated its 100th anniversary of statehood in 1989. Olympia was at the center of the celebration which featured over 3000 events state-wide. Pictured here is the kickoff event at the capitol grounds, held on November 11, 1988, to inaugurate the Centennial Year. Over 800 volunteers, coordinated by the Department of Natural Resources, formed an outline of the state and the number "100" with umbrellas. Photograph courtesy of the State Capital Museum, a division of the Washington State Historical Society

The Yashiro Japanese Garden located at the entrance to Olympia adjacent to City Hall was completed in 1990 after seven years of planning and development. The garden is an example of the hill and pond style of Japanese garden. It was designed by Seattle landscape architect Robert Murasi who was trained in Kyoto, Japan.

Built with the assistance of volunteers, the garden was a joint effort of the City of Olympia, the Olympia-Yashiro Sister City Association and the City of Yashiro, Japan. Granite lanterns in the park were donated by the City of Yashiro. Photograph by Eldon Marshall

Completed in the spring of 1996, the new Olympia Farmer's Market provides larger market space, covered food vendor accommodations, a stage for performances, a demonstration garden, playground, and restroom facilities. The market, which hosts 180 small businesses, is a joint project of the City of Olympia, the Port of Olympia, and the Farmer's Market Association. Photograph by Steve Vento

The Korean War Veterans Memorial was authorized in 1989 by the Washington State Legislature. The memorial, by artist Deborah Copenhaver Fellows, is a sculpture of three soldiers in rain gear huddled around a fire. Dedicated July 24, 1993, the memorial is the first sponsored by a state to the war. Photograph by Steve Borst, courtesy of Washington State General Administration

Lacey dedicated its new library on March 23, 1991. The idea of a Lacey library was suggested as early as 1962. After being located in storefronts for many years, the new library was the result of a concentrated effort of the community and city to build the structure. Over $750,000 of the $2 million cost of the 20,000-square-foot structure was raised through local contributions.

The sculpture "Sharing" which graces the front entry of the library was installed in 1993. The life-size bronze work by sculptor Judy Phipps depicts a grandmother and child sharing their love of reading while seated on a bench. The project was funded by the City of Lacey, Patrons of South Sound Cultural Activities (POSSCA), TCI Cablevision, and other donors. Photograph courtesy of the City of Lacey

1995 marked the 150th anniversary of the arrival of the first permanent American settlers, the Simmons-Bush Party, to the falls of the Deschutes River in October 1845. The City of Tumwater and the Tumwater Sesquicentennial Committee sponsored a variety of events and projects including formal opening and closing ceremonies, a video, history book, history conference, and time capsule in the new Tumwater Library. One of the most colorful events was the wagon train which was a part of the annual Tumwater Fourth of July Celebration. Photograph of the parade courtesy of Tumwater Parks Department

St. Martin's College commemorated its 100th anniversary in 1995 with a year-long series of events. More than 650 friends and alumni gathered September 11, 1995 at a party at St. Martin's Pavilion to commemorate the date of the school's founding. Photograph of St. Martin's President David Spangler at the gala September celebration by Paul Peck courtesy of St. Martin's College

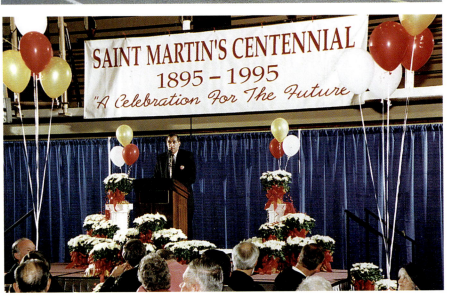

The grand opening of Intercity Transit's Olympia Transit Center was on August 28, 1994. The $5.35 million facility is the centerpiece of Intercity Transit's county-wide transportation system. The center includes a pedestrian transfer island with twelve bus bays, a customer service office, passenger seating, bicycle racks, public restrooms, and a landscaped park area.

The center features a multi-media public art installation called "Rain Forest." Elements of the work include a sixteen-panel glass mural, colored concrete in the shape of a rain forest plant, wrought-iron vortexes with wind chimes made from bus parts, eight colored acrylic and steel valances, and clay tiles. Photograph by Steve Vento

A Lacey audience is seen here enjoying part of the "In Tune" summer concert series in Thomas W. Huntamer Park at Woodland Square. The free concerts, co-sponsored by Lacey businesses, are part of many activities offered by the Lacey Parks and Recreation Department. Photograph courtesy of the Lacey Parks and Recreation Department

Bibliography

Between the Years 1895-1945. Lacey, Washington: St. Martin's College, n.d.

Blankenship, Mrs. George, comp. and ed. *Early History of Thurston County Washington.* Olympia: n.p., 1914.

Bowden, Angie Burt. *Early Schools of Washington Territory.* Seattle: Lowman and Hanford Co., 1935.

Hunt, Herbert. *Washington, West of the Cascades.* Chicago: The S. J. Clarke Publishing Co., 1917.

Jessett, Rev. Thomas Edwin, comp. *St. John's Church of Olympia (1853-1941).* n.p., n.d.

Miller, Wallace J. *Southwestern Washington.* Olympia: Pacific Publishing Co., 1890.

Newell, Gordon, ed. *The H. W. McCurdy Marine History of the Pacific Northwest from 1895.* Seattle: Superior Publishing Co., 1975.

Newell, Gordon. *Rogues, Buffoons & Statesmen.* Seattle: Superior Publishing Co., 1975.

Rathbun, John C. *History of Thurston County.* Olympia: n.p., 1895.

Schoenberg, Wilfred P., S. J. *A Chronicle of the Catholic History of the Pacific Northwest, 1743-1960.* Portland: Catholic Sentinel Printery, 1962.

Snowden, Clinton A. *A History of Washington.* New York: The Century History Co., 1909.

Steele, E. N. *The Rise and Decline of the Olympia Oyster.* Elma, Washington: Fulco Publications, 1957.

General References:

Clipping files of the Washington Room of the Washington State Library.

The *Daily Olympian, Washington Standard,* and *Olympia Tribune* back issues.

State Capital Museum files.

Index

A
Acme Brewery, 158
Aldred, Clayton, 65
Allen, George, 123
Armstrong, Oakie, 196
Ashley, Wilbur, 124
Ayer, Louise, 8, 68

B
Bailey Galzert (steamer), 110
Barnes, Burt, 117
Barnes, Claude, 117
Beaver (steamer), 108
Bellingham Bay Brewery, 158
Benoit, Joan, 229
Besse, Burt, 61
Besse, Charles
Bettman, Louis, 32
Bettman, Sig, 32
Bigelow House, 242
Bigelow, Daniel R., 38, 91
Biles, Clark, 24
Biles, Fannie, 158
Biles, James, 24, 25, 158
Black Hills Community Hospital, 230
Blom, Anna, 208
Borgens, Burt, 138
Boston Harbor, 74, 94, 95
Brenner Oyster Company, 74
Brey, Fred, 165
Bronson Motor Car Co., 138
Brown, Benjamin, 44
Brown, Mary Olney, 44
Budd, Thomas, 16
Burlingame, Isaac, 23
Burntrager Store, 60
Burntrager, Addie, 8, 68
Burntrager, Edith, 8, 68
Burntrager, Lizzie, 8, 68
Bush, George, 16, 20, 21, 34, 38
Bush, Henry, 21
Bush, Isabella, 21
Bush, Jackson, 21
Bush, Joseph, 21
Bush, Riley, 21
Bush, William O., 21, 57

C
Caledonia Hotel, 103
Camby, Marion, 179
Capital Brewing Company, 156, 158, 159, 160, 162-163, 166
Capital City Band, 70
Capital City (steamer), 109, 111
Capital Mall, 218, 222
Capitol Chevrolet, 184-185
Capitol Lake Interpretive Center, 227
Capitol Theater, 118, 135
Carlyon Addition, 89
Carlyon Avenue, 74
Carlyon Beach, 124
Carlyon Fairgrounds, 124
Carlyon, Fred, 124
Carlyon, P. H., 74, 118, 119
Cavanaugh, Rena, 8, 68
Centennial Brewing Company, 159
Centennial Station, 237
Central School, 58
Chambers Block, 86, 187
Chambers family, 40, 41
Chambers, A. H., 41, 74, 92
Chambers, David, 41, 128
Chambers, George, 41
Chambers, James, 41
Chambers, Letitia, 41
Chambers, Mary 41
Chambers, Thomas, 41
Chambers, Walter, 41
Chaplin, J. R., 91
Chilberg, Joe, 123
City of Aberdeen (steamer), 109
City of Olympia (aircraft), 131
City of Olympia (steamer), 11, 115, 131
City of Shelton (steamer), 110, 112
Cloverfields Farm, 126, 127, 205
Colfax, Greg, 241
Columbia Building, 61
Columbia Capital Medical Center, 230
Columbia Fire Engine, 123
Columbia Hall, 45, 50, 75, 97
Columbian, The (newspaper) 16
Conant, Elton, 116
Congregationalist Church, 35
Constitution (steamer), 108
Constitution, U.S.F., 186-188

Craig, Wiliam, 123
Crockett, Samuel B., 16
Crosby, Clanrick, 28, 29
Crosby, Nathaniel III, 28, 29, 50
Curtin, Ida, 61
Cusack, H., 65

D
de Lacey, O. C., 72
Department of Transportation, 155
Deschutes River, 158
DeVore, Rev. John F., 36
Doane, Captain Woodburg, 12, 54
Dofflemyer, 74, 94

E
Earthquake (1949), 187, 203
Earthquake (1965), 210
Eastman, Charles, 60
Eaton, Nathan, 56
Eld, Henry, 16
Eliza Anderson (steamer), 54, 109
Emilie Parker (schooner), 108
Emma Hayward (steamer), 109
Episcopal Church, 76
Evans, Elwood, 126

F
Fairy (steamer), 108
Farmer's Market, 226, 237, 248
Farquhar Store, 118, 147
Fauntleroy (steamer), 109
Ferguson, Jesse, 16, 18, 19
Ferry, Elisha P., 50, 51, 145
Filley, George E., 212
Fire department, 122
Fleetwood family, 41
Fort Eaton, 40, 56
Foy Store, 193
Foy, Ann, 193
Foy, Gordon, 193
Free, E. O., 65
Freedom Community, 40
French, John, 44
Frost, Filoy, 8, 68
Frost, Robert, 123
Funk, George, 100
Funk, Goldie Robertson, 100
Funk-Volland Building 100, 201

253

G

G. W. Kendall (brigantine), 108
Garfield School, 72, 81
Gelbach Flouring Mill, 27
Gelbach, Mr. and Mrs. George, 26, 27
Gold Bar Restaurant, 118, 144
Goldberg's, 68
Governor Elisha Ferry (steamer), 114
Governor's Mansion, 150
Greyhound (steamer), 109

H

Hale, Calvin, 62
Hale, Mrs. Pamela, 62, 72
Hamm's Brewery, 159
Harbor Days, 219, 230, 245
Harmon, Buck, 237
Harris, Gus, 65
Harris, I., 87
Harris, Mitchell, 87, 102
Hartley, Gov. Roland, 141-143
Hartsuck, Solie, 8, 68
Hawk, John Melvin, 44, 65
Hays, Smith, 23
Helm, Charles, 160
Henderson House Museum, 86, 226
Henry, D. S. B., 123
Highway-License Building, 206
Hillman, C. D., 94, 95
Hillside Inn, 164
Himes, Lestina, 56
Homann, Al, 201
Howard, Rebecca, 33
Hudson's Bay Company, 15, 16
Huggins, Mr. and Mrs. George, 83
Hunger march, 186, 190-191
Huntamer, Thomas W. Park, 251
Hunter, Emma, 61

I

Insurance Building, 151

J

Jeffers Studio, 120
Jeffers, Hugh, 131
Jeffers, Joseph, 120
Johnston, Clem, 123
Jones, Johnpaul, 241
June (brigantine), 108

K

Kane, Herb, 177
Kenney, Frank, 138, 166
KGY, 118, 119, 137, 187, 195, 196, 205, 206, 211
Kimball, Elizabeth, 232
Kindred, David, 16, 34
"Kiss, The" (sculpture), 236
Knights of Pythias, 65
Korean War Veterans' Memorial, 249
Krantz Hotel, 25

L

Labor and Industries Building, 239
Lacey Library, 250
Lacey Museum, 223
Lacey Music, Arts, Dance Festival, 218, 220
Lacey, 11, 41, 48, 49, 58, 72, 84, 85, 92, 119, 128, 133, 136, 137, 187, 193, 200, 208, 210-212, 218-220, 223, 224, 243, 250, 251
Lakefair, 200, 213, 219, 224, 225, 229, 233
Lange, Edward, 41, 74
Langlie, Arthur, 182
Lansdale, Anne, 8, 68
Lea Lumber, 93
Legislative Building, 151-155
Lemon, Millard, 212
Lewis and Clark Exposition, 159
Liberty Theater, 118, 134
Lincoln School, 72, 81, 118
Lincoln, Charles, 116
Little Hollywood, 186, 189
Littlejohn, Celia, 61
Lone Star Brewing Company, 159
Longhouse, Evergreen, 241
Lord, C. J., 77, 138, 196, 212

M

MacIntosh, Albert, 168
Major Tompkins (steamer), 108
Manville, Chester, 64
Marsh, Edmund, 33
Marshall, G. Eldon, 221
Marshville, 33, 48, 62, 218
Martin, Gov. Clarence, 94, 186, 192
Masonic Temple, 35, 88, 144, 146
Maxin, Ted, 193
McAllister, James, 16

McCarrogher, Joseph, 122
McClellan, John, 123
McClelland, Sam, 65, 123
McDowell, James, 212
McElroy, Harry, 138
McElroy, T. F., 16
McIntosh House, 86
McKenny Block (later Kneeland Hotel), 76, 86, 97, 160-161, 187
McKenny, Margaret, 200, 204
McKenny, T. I., 72, 76, 204
McMillan, Marcus 40, 41
Meares, Capt. John, 16
Methodist Church, the, 34, 36
Miller, William Winlock, 99, 205
Milroy, W. J., 75
Moore, A. W., 34
Moore, Mollie, 103
Mottman Building, 86, 97, 187, 201
Mottman, George, 102
Mountain View Golf Course, 128
Moyer, Maggie, 61
Multnomah (steamer), 95, 109, 110
Munn, Mrs. Mary, 61
Munson, A. J., 64
Murphy, John Miller, 42, 43, 73, 118, 123

N

National Guard, 75
New Market, 15
New Market Vocational Skills Center, 234-236
Nisqually (steamer), 109, 113
Nisqually, 15
Northern Light (steamer) 110
Northern Pacific Railroad, 165

O

O'Brien, Mrs. Fannie, 138
O'Conner, Michael, 66
O'Hares Store, 194
Oblates of Mary Immaculate, 16, 95
Oddfellows Hall, 50, 68
Old Betsy, 44
Old Capitol (Thurston County Courthouse), 72, 83, 119, 145, 147-149, 176
Old Port, 109

Olmsted Brothers, 145
Olympia, 11, 12, 16, 18, 22, 30, 32-39, 42, 44, 45, 48-50, 53, 54, 56, 58-62, 65, 66, 72, 78-81, 86-88, 90, 91, 94, 95, 98, 99, 106-109, 111, 113, 114, 118, 120-122, 124-130, 133, 140, 141, 144-147, 184, 188, 192, 193, 196, 197, 200, 201, 203, 205, 208-210, 212, 214, 218, 219, 221, 222, 224, 226-230, 232, 238, 247, 251
Olympia Brewery, 86, 95, 118, 156-183, 202, 226
Olympia Centennial, 198-199, 201, 202
Olympia Center, 232
Olympia City Hall, 208
Olympia Collegiate Institute, 91
Olympia Cornet Band, 50
Olympia Federal Savings, 212
Olympia Hotel, 70, 72, 88, 90
Olympia Isle Marina, 219, 227
Olympia Knitting Mills, 102
Olympia Light and Power Company, 72, 79, 80, 165, 177
Olympia Opera House, 73, 118
Olympia oysters, 54, 55, 61, 129
Olympia (ship), 163
Olympia Timberland Library, 53, 222
Olympia Transit Center, 251
Olympia-Tumwater Foundation, The, 158, 160, 183
Olympian Hotel, 127
Olympian (newspaper), 34, 83, 163, 1210, 218
Olympic Auto Camp, 132
Orbit (brigantine), 108
Ostrander, Dr. Nathaniel, 6, 52, 53, 68
Oyster Money, 186, 188

P
Pabst Brewing Company, 159, 160, 183
Pacific House, 33
Pagan Fest, 200, 210
Panorama City, 128, 201, 210
Patnude, Charles, 88
People's University, 91
Percival Dock, 74, 109, 115
Percival Landing Park, 221, 236, 244, 245
Percival, John C., 110, 192
Percival, Lurana Ware, 8, 37, 68

Percival, Samuel, 37, 109, 192
Pet Parade, 210
Pioneer Park, 240
Plamondon, Lois, 179
Port of Olympia, 130, 131, 187, 196, 197, 200, 204, 227, 230, 246
Port Townsend Brewery, 158
POSSCA, 218, 236
Presbyterian Church, 35
Priest Point Park, 95, 159, 186
Providence Academy, 49, 59, 88
Puget Sound Wesleyan Institute, 58, 91

R
Railroads, 48, 49, 62
Rainrunners, 229
Redpath, Catherine, 138
Reed, Mark E., 75, 112
Reed, T. M., 72, 120
Reinhart, C. S., 75
Rizbeck, Joe, 123
Robbins, Ed., 123
Roberts, Prof. W. H., 65
Rockway, Leland, 195
Roesch, Lewis Company, 162
Rogers, A. D., 96
Romaninski, Walt, 193
Root, Milo, 65
Rosenthal, Gustave, 61
Ruth, Fr. Sebastian, 119, 137

S
Sacred Heart Church, 133
Salem Brewery, 158
Sarah Warren (bark), 108
Schictwoot (scow), 108
Schmidt, Adolf "Bump" Jr., 183
Schmidt, Adolf Sr., 158, 178, 179, 180, 183
Schmidt, Clara Muench, 178
Schmidt, Frank, 160, 179
Schmidt, Frederick, 160, 179
Schmidt, Johanna Steiner, 159, 160, 178
Schmidt, Leopold F., Jr., 160, 178
Schmidt, Leopold F. "Rick," 183
Schmidt, Leopold F., Sr., 74, 95, 104, 156, 158, 159, 160, 162, 168, 178
Schmidt, Peter G., 158, 178, 179, 180, 182
Schmidt, Philippine, 160

Schmidt, Robert A. "Bobby," 183
Schmidt, Winnifred Lang, 183
Schofield, William, 123
Schupp, Henry, 160
Scully, Ed, 116
Semple, Gov. Eugene, 65
Senior-Community Center, 219, 232
Senna, James, 183
"Sharing" (sculpture), 250
Simila, Norma Jean, 179
Simmons, Christopher Columbus, 17
Simmons, Elizabeth Kindred, 15, 17
Simmons, Michael, 15, 16, 20, 28, 47
Sloan Shipyard, 118, 128
Smith, Ida B., 96
Smith, Levi Lathrop, 16, 22
Snyder, Frank, 65
Sol G. Simpson (steamer), 107, 108, 112
South Puget Sound Community College, 221
South Sound Center, 201, 211, 212
Springer, Charles H., 102, 138, 212
St. Martin's, 11, 74, 92, 93, 119, 136, 187, 208, 218, 223, 250
St. Peter Hospital, 49, 59, 118, 133, 216-217, 242-243
Stack, Howard, 177
State Capital Museum, 196, 236
Stevens, Hazard, 80, 126, 127, 205, 207
Stevens, Isaac Ingalls, 18, 49, 144, 145
Stevens, Margaret Lyman, 39
Stewart, John, 122
Stuart, Mrs. A. H., 49, 72, 98
Sunset Life Insurance Co., 124, 209
Sunset Telephone-Telegraph, 50
Sylvester Park, 78, 118, 125, 139, 200, 218, 232
Sylvester, Clara, 22
Sylvester, Edmund, 16, 18, 22, 59, 78, 108, 144

T
T. J. Potter (steamer), 109
Talcott, Charles, 123, 138
Talcott, Grant, 122, 138
Telephone Exchange, 138
Temple of Justice, 150
Three-Meter, 132, 167, 168
Thurston County Courthouse (1900) 88; (1930) 186; (1977) 218, 222

255

Tivoli Fountain, 158, 182, 204
Toklas & Kaufman, 60, 61
Transportation Building, 154
Traveler (steamer), 108
Trosper family, 132
Troy, P. M., 212
Tumwater City Hall, 245
Tumwater Falls Park, 159, 174, 207
Tumwater Hall, 74, 104
Tumwater Historic Park, 175, 227
Tumwater Sesquicentennial, 250
Tumwater, 11, 16, 18, 19, 23-25, 28-30, 48, 49, 52, 60, 72, 79, 80, 86, 93, 104, 124, 131, 132, 180-181, 194, 195, 200, 207, 215, 218, 219, 226, 227, 238-239, 240, 245, 250
Tunin, May, 61
Turner, Henry C., 193
Tyee Motor Inn, 220

U
Union Academy, 55, 91
Union Mills, 72, 84, 85, 200

V
Valiton, Pierre, 159
Van Epps Music, 66
Van Epps, Arly, 138
Vancouver, Capt. George, 16
Venus (steamer), 107, 108
Vietnam Veterans' Memorial, 244
Volland, Addie, 100

W
Wallace Hotel, 25
Ward Shipyards, 128
Ward, Ira, 23
Washington Center for the Performing Arts, 134, 218, 231
Washington School, 72, 81
Washington State Centennial, 236, 247
Washington Veneer, 119, 130, 203
Watershed Park, 221
Weller, William, 122
Western Metalcraft, 182
Whitworth, Rev. George, 35
Wilbur, Andy, 241
Wilder and White, 145, 154, 187
Wilkes, Lt. Charles, 16
Willey Navigation, 110, 111

Willey, Sam, 110
William Winlock Miller High School, 99, 125, 205
Williams, Charles, 60
Willie, S. S. (steamer), 110
Wilson G. Hunt (steamer), 109
Wohleb, Joseph, 120, 125, 135, 184, 186, 196, 208
Wohleb, Robert, 201, 208
Wolf, A. W., 160
Women's Club, 98, 103, 132, 222
Women's Olympic Marathon Trials, 219, 228-229
Wood family, 49
Wood, Dick, 123
Wood, Isaac, 41, 74
Woodland, 11, 48, 49, 72, 75
Woodruff Building, 49, 50, 66, 67, 86
Woodruff, Sam, 66
World War I Memorial, 154
Wright, Alex, 122
Wright, Bert, 65

Y
Yantis, Eliza Jane, 52
Yashiro Japanese Garden, 247
Yosemite (steamer) 95, 113

Z
Zabel family, 135

Olympia, Tumwater, and Lacey

a pictorial history

by Shanna B. Stevenson